LOST SOPRIS

LOST
SOPRIS

GENEVIEVE FAORO-JOHANNSEN
AND ROBERT D. VIGIL JR.

Foreword by Tom Potter, Trinidad Carnegie Public Library

THE
History
PRESS

Published by The History Press
Charleston, SC
www.historypress.com

First published 2024

Manufactured in the United States

ISBN 9781467154130

Library of Congress Control Number: 2023950812

Notice: The information in this book is true and complete to the best of our knowledge. It is offered without guarantee on the part of the author or The History Press. The author and The History Press disclaim all liability in connection with the use of this book.

With gratitude to my parents and grandparents, whose love of photos and photography captured history almost unknowingly as they went about their daily lives. Thank you for the legacy of photos and documents that you preserved. Without family available to tell me about the photos, I am eternally grateful to the friends they grew up with who knew the people in the photos when I did not.

G.F.J.

For my wife, who has always been there to encourage me to follow my passion and reach beyond. For my grandparents and parents, who saved the memorabilia of our past.

R.D.V.

CONTENTS

PRELUDE

SOPRIS

By Crist D. Cunico
Sydney, Australia
March 18, 1981
On letterhead from Hotel Shilla, Seoul, Korea

Oh, how I long for the days of old
When folks were simple and their word was gold.

I'm on my last leg of a six-country tour
But I'd rather be back in Sopris where things were pure.

I've seen a lot over the last thirty years
But for dear old Sopris I still shed tears.

Sopris is gone forever now
But get her out of me, I don't know how.

Those beautiful people I still see now
It was common courtesy and respect without a bow.

The tender memories I will cherish to my grave
Where people were honest and the miners, brave.

That quality of life was indeed unique
And to modern thinking it be thought antique.

But to those of us who experienced that simple life
We were tender, loving, caring, and without serious strife.

What saddens me most from this whole ordeal
Is to know that when we're gone it will not have been for real.

That wonderful heritage, love, and quality of life
Will not be part of the next generation's guiding life.

Oh, Sopris with your tender people so dear
Laying fallow under water and soon no one will hear.

To those of us who were born and grew up there
We'll all go to our maker with something to share.

We were lucky to have experienced that simple life
And it will guide us safely until we see eternal life.

Crist Donald Cunico was the son of Cristiano Cunico and Mary (Pena) Ferri Cunico, residents of Jerryville. Crist Donald excelled as a student and athlete in school at Sopris, and after completing his degree, he went on to enjoy a career with General Electric in its medical equipment division. His career took him all over the world, and while in Germany, he met and married his wife, Nora Hinkle. They raised four children, Christina, Crist K., Sandra and Lisa, and we are extremely grateful to Crist for his archives and to Christina for locating and sharing her dad's thoughts.

FOREWORD

One of my responsibilities at the Trinidad Public Library is overseeing the library's History Room, an archive of local history of Las Animas County. People from all over the United States visit the History Room to find information about ancestors who lived in Trinidad or in the twenty-some coal camps that sprang up during the coal mining boom in Southern Colorado. We have a drawer full of files, each file devoted to one of the coal camps. Those camp towns are mostly gone now. When the local coal industry all but disappeared, the coal companies removed anything of value. Towns whose populations were once measured in the thousands are nothing but a few building foundations now. There are exceptions—towns where a few people still live. But places like Hastings, Berwind, Delagua, Tollerburg, Gray Creek, Engleville and Morley are long gone. I said that each coal camp has its own file in the drawer, but there is an exception: Sopris has five file folders.

This book, written by and for former Sopris residents and their descendants, is a testament to the fact that Sopris lives on in the hearts of the people who lived there. The five smaller communities that made up what became known as Sopris are now also gone, submerged when the U.S. Army Corps of Engineers built a flood control dam in the early 1970s to calm the occasionally fearsome Purgatoire River. Somehow, although much of the town is now underwater, gone forever, these people still see themselves as part of a living Sopris community. Perhaps it has something to do with the fact that the end was predicted and that their emigration was forced. Perhaps it is because they made their great sacrifice knowing that it benefitted the many, and that it had to be done. Perhaps it is the eerie vision of a town trapped underwater and frozen in time. I don't know the reasons, but I do know that there is something very different about being from Sopris.

I hope you enjoy reading about the people and places of Sopris as much as I did. This book describes in detail all the players, from the individual and corporate land and mine owners to the miners and their families and the second and third generations of people who grew up there and owned or frequented the stores, restaurants, bars and baseball fields and who attended and taught in the schools. It also includes that equally important Sopris character: the Purgatoire River.

Tom Potter
Trinidad Public Library
August 2023

ACKNOWLEDGEMENTS

This book came about because of the people who made Sopris home, creating a cohesive and deeply intertwined community with smaller unique neighborhoods that began around the many mines in this coal-rich area. Through friendships, marriages and employment, strong bonds formed and continue from generation to generation. The physical homes of Sopris are gone, but the land remains, and former residents return to the land again and again to remember and celebrate who we are because of where we were raised. Our traditions, our faith, our foods and the games that our ancestors brought from their homelands became known to all and continue to be part of our celebrations. We are indebted to our parents and grandparents, who shared their stories and celebrated the traditions of our heritages. We are indebted to all who once lived in Sopris and her neighborhoods and who have provided us with photos, facts and folklore certain to trigger memories possibly forgotten.

We also acknowledge our fellow historians—the librarians, curators and businesses—who oversee and keep safe the original photos, documents and maps that provide irrefutable evidence of our past. Special thanks to the Carnegie Libraries of Trinidad and Boulder; Pikes Peak Library District; Denver Public Library's Western History Digital Collection; History Colorado's Archives; Bessemer Historical Society–Steelworks Center of the West and the Colorado Fuel and Iron Company Archives; Pueblo City and County Library's Western History Collection; the Western Museum of Mining and Industry; and Frank Images in Trinidad.

We gratefully acknowledge our fellow researchers and authors who have dug deeply and verified additional facts that support our research and add depth to our understanding of specific topics, as well as the many families that shared their history with us through photographs and family archives.

INTRODUCTION

On a road map of Colorado printed before 1970, a small dot identifies Sopris, located adjacent to State Highway 12 and approximately five miles southwest of Trinidad. While treated as one entity, that small community, part of the Southern Colorado coalfields, was a composite of six unique neighborhoods along the path of the Purgatoire River. One main road, Dexter Street, ran through the town from east to west, allowing entrance to the neighborhoods from three access routes. One route involved coming in from Starkville, to the south, and entering the main road as it passed by Piedmont, and a second access was possible directly from Highway 12, just beyond Jansen, and involved crossing the original trolley bridge, known to us as the "Blasi Bridge" (thus named because it crossed the Purgatoire Rive by the Blasi farm). A third access was to the west of the town near Long Canyon, and it required crossing the Purgatoire River and train tracks near the trestle by Sopris Plaza. When entering there, you continued along the road to the left as it made its way into town, arriving at the west end of Dexter Street. While this is a story about a town, it is also a story about a river—a river that provided irrigation to the farmers, water for the steam engines and washeries of the mines and a source of adventure to the young—a river that ultimately proved to be both a blessing and the reason the dot on the map disappeared.

The neighborhoods, each within a mile of Main Sopris, began around privately owned mines and mines owned by the Denver Fuel Company, the Rocky Mountain Fuel Company and, later, the Colorado Fuel and Iron

With the mines isolated in the foothills and canyons of the Purgatoire River, the Trinidad Electric Company saw an opportunity to expand its customer base and create more business for Trinidad merchants by extending its lines from the city into the camps. Trinidad Electric Company took possession of the bridge to the northeast of St. Thomas (later known to locals as the Blasi Bridge) from the contractors on March 2, 1904. *Photo courtesy of History Colorado, Stephen H. Hart Research Center.*

Company. Many of the independent mines sold out to the predecessors of the Colorado Fuel and Iron Company and became part of that corporation when the mergers took place. The neighborhoods—Piedmont, Jerryville (also recorded as Farrelleville), St. Thomas, Sopris Canyon and Main Sopris— came to be because of the nearby mines, while Sopris Plaza (formerly known as Lavese Plaza, for the Lave family that first resided there) began as a series of farms along the river. In government documents (such as the census) and city directories, all the neighborhoods often fall under the umbrella term *Sopris* but are often identifiable by the notes of the enumerator that indicate the name of the street being recorded or by a note at the top of the page that identifies the specific neighborhood (on census records). To determine just where people were located within the town is difficult for those not sufficiently familiar with the area. Alfred Laiminger published a book of historic maps, available through the Trinidad Historical Society, to help address this need, and maps in Appendix D show the final owners as buyouts occurred.

Families were bonded within their neighborhoods and also as a community, coming together for work, worship, music, school and sports. The oldest community members had arrived from various European

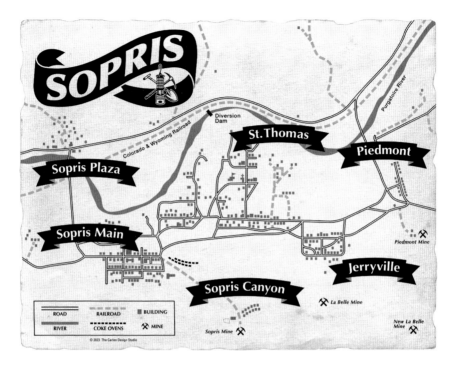

The neighborhoods of Sopris came to be because of the agricultural lands near the Purgatoire River and the very productive coal seam that is in the area and continues to the north and west. This map approximates the neighborhoods and does not specify the exact number of homes and blocks within each neighborhood. *Map courtesy of the Carleo Design Studio, Pueblo, Colorado.*

regions, often with a few friends or with siblings and other relatives from the same town. Others came a bit later, after they received letters from those who had gone before them telling of the camps and their new lives. Other residents came north to the United States from Mexico, often settling in New Mexico before entering the Colorado Territory. As the world advanced, access to the area improved and settlement increased. Six things played important roles in bringing people to the area and establishing a community: the Santa Fe Trail (1821–80), the Maxwell Land Grant (1841–1942), the "Rush to the Rockies" that followed the discovery of gold near Pike's Peak (1859), the Civil War (1861–65), the Homestead Act (1862) and the arrival of the Santa Fe Railroad in Trinidad (1878). All six brought people into Trinidad and created interest in the nearby outlying areas, including the area that became the neighborhoods of Sopris. Main Sopris was officially established in 1889 and existed for just under eighty years. Other neighborhoods began a bit earlier or a bit later, but all faced the same fate in 1968 as their homes and properties were purchased by the U.S. government to make way for a dam and reservoir.

Elbridge Bright Sopris came to Colorado with his family when the land was still part of the Kansas Territory. His father had come to what is now the Denver metro area to help establish the town of Auraria and to seek gold as part of the gold rush of 1859.[1] Both Elbridge and his father served in the Civil War, with Elbridge having the good fortune of being in Southern Colorado and Northern New Mexico.[2] Familiarity with these areas served him well for many years as a businessman and politician.[3] He never resided in the neighborhoods of Sopris, yet one neighborhood is named after him, and his influence significantly impacted the coal industry in the area.

By the late 1800s, a race was on to create the railroads necessary to move the products of the entrepreneurial wealthy—the robber barons—and their influence reached west.[4] In September 1878, the Santa Fe Railroad reached Trinidad, linking the area and its resources to new opportunities near and far as steel became important and the United States' leaders of industry required local coal to fuel their companies and their ambitions. Trains changed the world, and that river changed the trains, washing away the tracks and paralyzing commerce in its wake for decades. Because of those floods, it also changed Sopris—forever.

PART I

ELBRIDGE BRIGHT SOPRIS

FOUNDING FATHER, SOLDIER, STATESMAN, SCOUNDREL AND STRATEGIC OPPORTUNIST

Chapter 1

ARRIVAL IN 1859

An ambitious young man from a family with newfound social status during westward expansion, Elbridge Bright Sopris arrived in Colorado as a seventeen-year-old and remained a person of interest and influence for the next seventy-five years—years that strongly influenced the development of Las Animas County and the state of Colorado.[5]

IN HIS FATHER'S FOOTSTEPS—AND THEN NOT

To talk about Elbridge B. Sopris, we must first introduce his father, Richard Sopris, who—in just a bit over a year's time—moved into the western front of the Kansas Territory and established towns; filed mining claims; discovered a historic group of hot springs, now known as Glenwood Springs; and had a nearby mountain, previously unidentified, named Mount Sopris in his honor.[6] As Elbridge watched his father's success, he saw the path to his future.

Richard arrived in Auraria (a precursor to Denver) in March 1859 and became one of the original shareholders, prior to going on to coauthor a draft constitution and city laws for Denver. Caught up in the "Race to the Rockies," Richard filed mining claims along the Platte River and in Gilpin County. During that time of claim jumpers and cutthroat competition for Colorado's hidden bounties, a Miners' Union was formed to maintain law and order and establish laws to govern mining claims. Richard Sopris was elected president of the Miners' Union. His reputation as a civic leader and person of character led to his being elected to represent Arapaho County in the Kansas legislature during the fall of 1859. His accolades as a public servant continued through a second term of the territorial legislature, in which he served as sergeant-at-arms, and he was a delegate to the first constitutional convention of Colorado. Sopris became the first city council president for Denver and continued in local government as sheriff, deputy sheriff, mayor and park commissioner from 1864 to 1890. During the Civil War, he was appointed as captain in Company C, First Colorado Cavalry for one year.[7]

In addition to his local reputation in Arapaho County, in the summer of 1860, he continued to collaborate with others to survey and map this new part of the country and to note the natural resources, both aboveground and in the depths of the earth.

Elbridge Bright Sopris came to Colorado in 1859 at age seventeen and first came to Southern Colorado and Northern New Mexico during the Civil War. He returned in 1867 as a businessman and maintained ties with the area throughout his life. *Photo courtesy of History Colorado, Stephen H. Hart Research Center.*

His father's almost spontaneous climbing of the ladder of success within Arapaho County and Denver society served young Elbridge and the family well, and they were welcomed to dinners and galas hosted by the local elite. E.B. met people of influence and other ambitious young men to build futures with, knowing that collaboration had served his father well and could serve him well also. Elbridge made choices that would influence his destiny.[8]

THE CIVIL WAR YEARS

Elbridge began his military career on November 1, 1862, as an enlisted member of Colorado's First Cavalry, Company A, at the rank of corporal.[3] His fight to turn the Texans back at the Battle of Glorieta Pass in New

Mexico turned out to be an event that was recognized above many others for the rest of his life—in part because he outlived every other member of that engagement.[9]

Elbridge reenlisted on August 20, 1864, as a second lieutenant in the Third Cavalry, Company A (before transferring to Company H) and served under Colonel John Chivington during what were known as the Indian Uprisings. A notable event during that enlistment was the Battle of Sand Creek, fought on November 29 and November 30, 1864, near Eads, Colorado. In reviewing the encounter, those in authority deemed it to have been a massacre, in part because of the number of women and children who died. The site of the massacre is now managed by the National Park Service and listed as the Sand Creek Massacre National Historic Site. The company disbanded on December 28, 1864; by then, Elbridge was a first lieutenant. He represented the Third Regiment of the Colorado Cavalry at the signing of the treaty between the United States government and the Tabeguache band of Utah Indians, which was signed by President Lincoln on December 14, 1864, in Washington, D.C.[10]

PUBLIC AND PRIVATE LIFE

After mustering out of the military in 1864, Elbridge returned to the Denver area to work locally and spoke of returning to the area of Southern Colorado and New Mexico where he had served, mentioning a desire to open a billiards saloon in Trinidad. In July 1867, he pursued that path, establishing the Exchange Billiards Saloon at the corner of C Street and Main, renting space from John Skelly, a local businessman.[11]

While living in Trinidad, Elbridge was called into service in many capacities, governmentally and politically. In 1873, he was appointed deputy United States surveyor for the Territories of Colorado and New Mexico.[12] In 1874, he became inspector general under territorial governor Elbert.[13] In 1877, he was promoted to the rank of brigadier general of the second division of the state militia by Governor Routt.[14] In 1882, Elbridge joined the Colorado House of Representatives and went on to retain that position for a second term.[15] From 1886 to 1888, General Sopris captained a local (Trinidad) hose team that competed with other fire brigades throughout the state to prove who was most effective in responding to local fires.[16]

Chapter 2

ENTREPRENEURIAL ENDEAVORS

O fficially residing in Trinidad and continuing to build cohesion through organizations like the Trinidad Hose Team, Elbridge came to know the people of the community. Since the governmental positions he held were somewhat part time, he was able to pursue long-term ambitions of wealth on the side. He was in Denver and Golden, the capital of Colorado until 1876 when Colorado achieved statehood,[17] a significant amount of the time. He often worked with local partners in his business dealings. One such person was William Littlefield, owner of a local book and stationery shop, who collaborated with E.B. in acquiring coal lands that became the Sopris mine.

Through his work as the deputy United States surveyor in Southern Colorado and Northern New Mexico, Elbridge developed a thorough knowledge of the land and its resources—but never reported the mineral wealth of the land in the documentation he submitted to the government. Knowing the wealth of the land, Elbridge and William Littlefield filed a land patent for 320 acres of Las Animas County coal land in the Township 33 South and the Range 64 West in the early 1880s.[18] Others, who could not be located thereafter, filed petitions for the adjacent coal lands in that township and range—this farce was a way of accessing more land by making up pretend filers who could never be found, other than one who testified that none of the others ever existed or lived on the land.[19] In April 1887, Acting Secretary Muldrow recommended to the attorney general that a suit should be filed to cancel twenty homestead patents and recover the rich coal

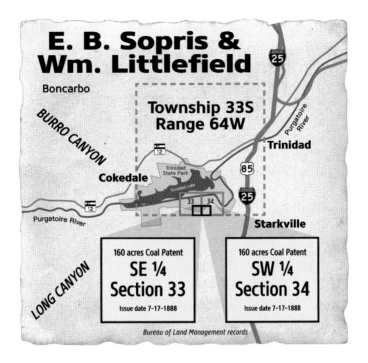

It was a well-kept secret, until it wasn't. During his Civil War years, and as deputy United States surveyor in 1873, Elbridge B. Sopris discovered the mineral wealth of the land in Las Animas County. As deputy United States surveyor for the area, he was required to document the natural resources of the land he surveyed, but he did not. When General William Jackson Palmer built a steel mill to the north in Pueblo, Sopris and a partner filed a patent for 320 acres of the richest coal land in the county. *Map courtesy of the Carleo Design Studio, Pueblo, Colorado.*

land.[20] As a Civil War veteran, Elbridge was in possession of Porterfield scrip, certificates specifically issued to veterans to enable them to purchase public land not available to those who did not serve.[21] Aware of Muldrow's recommendation to try to get the lands back, in 1887, Elbridge used the rights and privileges of the Porterfield scrip to obtain the land as a way to prevent it from being taken from him.[22]

In the April 16, 1875 edition of the *Trinidad Enterprise*, a small ad tells of Elbridge teaming up with Ed Bright to remain in the area and continue as a surveyor. Elbridge created the plat for the first Trinidad neighborhoods, and the two of them advertised their ability to locate and survey ranches and provide reliable information regarding the location of coal land or timber land. Those years as deputy United States surveyor continued to be valuable.

SURVEYORS
BRIGHT & SOPRIS

Surveyors. Locate ranches and attend to Surveying generally. Township and City Plats always on hand. Parties desiring to locate coal or timber land can get reliable information by calling or writing to us.[23]

By 1888, the Sopris mine had been sold to the Denver Fuel Company, which established the Main Sopris neighborhood;[24] then, in turn, the Denver Fuel Company sold the mines and town to the Colorado Fuel Company and General William Jackson Palmer a year later. In 1892, the mine became part of the merger of the Colorado Fuel Company and the Colorado Coal and Iron Company to create the Colorado Fuel and Iron Company.[25]

In 1893, E.B. Sopris was called on to testify in a lawsuit between the Maxwell Land Grant Company and the Colorado Fuel Company regarding lands he had once owned; each company believed they had ownership of it. In his testimony, he stated,

> *I once owned these tracts of land. I have been on them frequently. I think I was first on them about 1869, but to know them as those subdivisions of the sections was when I made the survey in 1873, and ran the exterior lines of the section, and camped on Raton Creek, that runs through this quarter section....Between 1878 and 1887 there was one man on the land part of the time that I told to go on and mine some coal, and the only other man that occupied the ground during that time, to my recollection, was a man put there by R.J. Wooton, who established a temporary toll gate there, on his toll road....The man I sent there to dig coal did not reside on the land.*[26]

For many years, E.B. maintained a residence in Denver and lodged in Trinidad. Even though his time spent in Trinidad each year was diminishing, in 1910, he became alderman for the First Ward of Trinidad, devoting a good deal of his efforts toward keeping dance halls that were open to the public from corrupting young women through exposure to unsavory males; these efforts were a cornerstone of his service. By that time, the Exchange Billiards Salon had become a dance hall under a different proprietor. By 1913, Elbridge had stepped on enough toes that, although a lifelong Republican, he ran for reelection as an independent. His business sense served him and Trinidad well for several terms.[27]

John Skelly died in 1879; ten years later, Elbridge married his widow, Mary Louise St. Vrain Skelly, who was then residing in Denver. He later adopted her son and daughter, giving them the surname Sopris and causing much confusion in historical records. Mary died of "a tumor of the throat" after a six-week illness at the age of sixty-eight.[28]

WILLIAM LITTLEFIELD, A.K.A. W.A. MORRILL

As we look at the questionable behaviors of Elbridge B. Sopris, we may begin to wonder about William Littlefield, his co-applicant for coal lands. We do not know how or when they met, but it does seem that William Littlefield also had a history of indiscretions and that he and E.B. Sopris were, as they say, "birds of a feather."

William Littlefield made Trinidad his permanent residence in the late 1870s, opening a book and stationery store and collaborating with Sopris in filing land patents for the coalfields that became Sopris. At the time of his death, it was verified that William Littlefield was, in fact, William A. Morrill, a former paymaster with the Missouri Kansas & Texas Railroad who went missing from Sedalia, Missouri, on September 22, 1878.

Newspaper coverage regarding the disappearance of William A. Morrill, age thirty-nine, speaks of him being distraught and haggard in appearance and recounts that he had been complaining of suffering from terrible pain

William Littlefield came to Trinidad from Sedalia, Missouri, where he had been employed as the paymaster for the Missouri Kansas & Texas Railroad Company until his disappearance on September 29, 1878. He owned a book and stationery shop in Trinidad and partnered with Elbridge B. Sopris to apply for a 320-acre land patent that became the first Sopris mine. *Photo courtesy of History Colorado, Stephen H. Hart Research Center.*

in his head for a period of two months. Morrill mentioned that a doctor in Hannibal, Missouri, had advised him to go west to Colorado for his health, predicting that his condition would be fatal if he remained in Missouri. In addition, it came to light at the time of his disappearance that Morrill was short in his accounts, with $4,500 unaccounted for. When he could not be found, a search party was organized, and as he was well known and well liked, over one hundred people joined the search, but to no avail.[29]

Leaving his wife and children without a farewell of any kind, Morrill seems to have changed clothes in the middle of the night and then purchased a train ticket at four thirty in the morning, leaving all remnants of his former life behind. Had he not chosen Trinidad, a major hub of train travel, his secret may have never come to light, but because so many people traveled through Trinidad and spent time there as it became renowned for its culture and commerce, two years after Morrill's disappearance, his whereabouts were revealed when a man visited from Sedalia and encountered him, going by the name of Littlefield. A second man from Sedalia also encountered Morrill several months later, and the people of Sedalia believed what they heard of Morrill's whereabouts, but there was no attempt to return him to Sedalia.[30] Morrill did return to Missouri in 1883 but not to Sedalia. He returned to Lexington, Missouri, to visit and then marry a young woman from that town who knew him only as Mr. Littlefield, having become acquainted with him in Trinidad; she then accompanied him back to Trinidad as his wife.[31]

PART II

THE NEIGHBORHOODS

Chapter 1

SOPRIS PLAZA

ounded as a farming community rather than a mining community, on the north side of the Purgatoire River, Sopris Plaza would have been far from the property damage of the 1913–14 strike conflicts had it not been for the train tracks and the trestle adjacent to the neighborhood, which were targeted by the strikers. Unlike other neighborhoods of Sopris, Sopris Plaza had no saloons, churches or general stores. Children from Sopris Plaza were bused to school and often attended St. Thomas School during the elementary grades, but arrangements could be made for them to attend Lincoln School in Main Sopris if a small tuition was paid.[32] The Colorado Fuel and Iron Company financially supported one school in each camp for the children of the miners, and Lincoln School in Main Sopris was that school.

The earliest settlers included Rafael, Manuel and Miguel Lave. Rafael's land petition for 120 acres was finalized and granted on September 8, 1891, by President Benjamin Harrison. The Lave name was reflected in the community for many years, and the entire community was referred to as Lavese Plaza—but noted as La Vata Plaza in the sidebars of the 1910 census.

Because the demand for coal is somewhat seasonal, it was not uncommon for men to farm during the spring and summer months and then work in the mines after harvest. Both the Cuccia and Blasi families lived in Sopris Plaza and had farms along the banks of the Purgatoire River. Because of the unpredictable nature of the river, there were years of crop loss—and even the loss of animals as floods washed through. One story told by Anthony

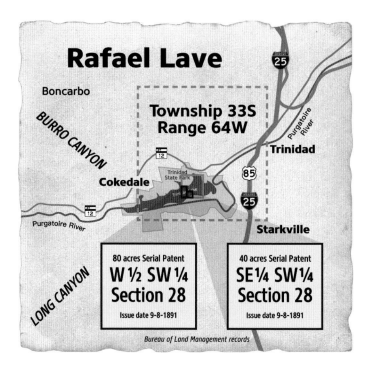

North of the Purgatoire River, Rafael Lave's land was the beginning of what was initially known as Lavese Plaza and then became Sopris Plaza. It was not coal land, but access to the river's waters made it very productive farmland. Other families homesteaded nearby, and a series of "truck farms" produced vegetables and fruits that were sold locally and shipped to other markets. *Map courtesy of the Carleo Design Studio, Pueblo, Colorado.*

Blasi is of a spring flood that took out fencing in its path and washed away animals. Small piglets were located floating along in the river in Trinidad, and it was determined that they had traveled the entire five miles from Sopris Plaza, buoyantly riding the waves as the flood moved through each town on its way to Trinidad.

Giuseppe and Vita Cuccia arrived in the United States in 1887 from Palazzo Adriano, Sicily, with their young family, during the time that the coalfields of the area were being developed. In 1910, their family included five children, three sons and two daughters. They established a goat farm and raised crops, and their son Frank continued to operate the family farm until he was required to sell it to the U.S. government in 1968 to make way for the dam and reservoir. Frank married Mary Niccoli in 1932, and together they raised four sons on the land, Joe, Mike, John and Jim.

The Cuccia farm was along the Purgatoire River close to the train trestle. Giuseppe and Vita Cuccia arrived in the United States in 1887 from Palazzo Adriano, Sicily, with their young family. They established a goat farm and raised crops, and their son Frank (*above*) and his family farmed the land until they were required to sell it to the U.S. government in 1968 to make way for the dam and reservoir. *Photo courtesy of Robert Cuccia and Cuccia Family Photo Archives.*

Joe Cuccia acquires an enthusiastic helper for the day: his son Jim. Horses were the easiest way to access the challenging terrain of the hillsides, and they were ridden for pleasure as well. Within the Cuccia family, all began to ride at a young age, and they passed that heritage on to the next generation. A well-trained horse was essential, and this one was no exception, standing quietly as Jim hitches a ride to the next stop. *Photo courtesy of Robert Cuccia and Cuccia Family Photo Archives.*

Chaps and a good pair of boots were essential protection when riding through low-to-the-ground junipers and patches of scrub oak. When you're as tall as Mike, John and Joe Cuccia were, they even protect you from the cacti you might encounter as you walk the farm to tend the livestock. Having a good and faithful dog was like having another set of eyes to alert you to danger, which might take the form of a rattlesnake or another threat. *Photo courtesy of Robert Cuccia and Cuccia Family Photo Archives.*

Shared grandparents all around! The Antista-Cimino children grew up next door to each other, as cousins and almost as siblings. Tony and Fay became the parents of six children (with the addition of Theresa after this photo was taken), and Joe and Frances were the parents of four (Joey arrived after this photo was taken). *Back row, left to right*: Bart (son of Tony and Fay), Elizabeth Fay (daughter of Tony and Fay), Bart (son of Joe and Frances). *Middle row, left to right*: Mary (daughter of Tony and Fay), Elizabeth Josephine (daughter of Joe and Frances). *Front row, left to right*: Domenic and John (sons of Tony and Fay), Mary Rose (daughter of Joe and Frances). *Photo courtesy of Elizabeth Antista DelMonte and Antista-Cimino Family Photo Archives.*

Opposite, bottom: Pictured are the Antista brothers and the Cimino sisters. Tony Antista married Fay Cimino, and Joe Antista married Frances Cimino in a double wedding ceremony. The Antista parents, Bart and Elizabeth, came to the United States from Cefalu, on the northern coast of Sicily, in 1891. By 1920, Bart and Elizabeth were the parents of five children. In April 1926, their son Tony married Fay Cimino, and their son Joe married her sister, Frances Cimino. Between the two families, Bart and Elizabeth were loved by ten grandchildren who grew up in nearby homes. *Photo courtesy of Elizabeth Antista DelMonte and Antista-Cimino Family Photo Archives.*

Sopris Plaza was also home to the Bart and Elizabeth Antista family, who came to the United States from Cefalu, on the north coast of Sicily, in 1891. By 1920, Bart and Elizabeth were the parents of five children, two of whom would remain in Sopris Plaza and raise their own children there. In April 1926, Tony Antista married Fay Cimino, and Joe Antista married her sister, Frances Cimino. Their children grew up next door to each other, side by side as cousins and almost as siblings. Following the tradition of naming the firstborn of each gender after the grandparents, each family had a Bart and an Elizabeth, making it necessary to use a nickname or add an adjective to clarify who was being spoken of—tall Bart or short Bart, Lizzie or Ella.

The 1910 census refers to the area as Plaza Lavata and records the residents as members of three "pueblos" within the neighborhood, with ten families in the first pueblo, seven in the second and eleven in the third. Most residents were born in Italy, New Mexico and Colorado, with Louis and Frank Alishio having been born in Louisiana—New Orleans was the port of entry frequently used by families coming to the United States from Sicily, and they often resided there for a few years before moving to other states.

Chapter 2

SOPRIS CANYON

When people spoke of living "up the canyon," they were referring to a valley between the foothills where many homes for the miners, and a home for the mine superintendent, were built. Companies were contracted to construct rows of homes that were sometimes divided into "flats" that housed a family on each level and sometimes simpler four-room cottages for individual families. In addition, the company would rent company land to the miners for as little as a dollar a year, and the miners could construct a residence on the property. In 1910, the census enumerator made a note in the margin indicating that people were living "some all together, and others in sheds or dugouts" on the hillsides between Sopris Canyon and Jerryville.

The Colorado Fuel and Iron Company encouraged the miners to care for their homes and to beautify them by establishing both flower and vegetable gardens, rewarding their efforts with an opportunity to earn cash rewards. The publication *Camp and Plant* came out each month between December 1901 and April 1904, sharing updates on what was happening at each coal camp and presenting ideas and information intended to make the lives of the miners and their families better. One article emphasized how vines could enhance the look of a simple home, and as archival photos of Sopris Canyon homes indicate, the miners took that to heart. Some vines were purely ornamental, and others were fruit-bearing, yielding squash and gourds.

Modern homes were constructed to replace the small adobe homes in the foothills of Sopris Canyon around 1916. Some homes were single-family dwellings, and others were multifamily dwellings with one family on each level. All included an outhouse behind the home. *Photo courtesy of Steelworks Center of the West, Bessemer Historical Society, Pueblo, Colorado.*

Little Italy was created on the hillsides between Sopris Canyon and Jerryville on land leased from the mining company for as little as one dollar per year. When the census enumerator saw the community, she was seemingly dismayed by its ramshackle appearance and noted in a margin that the people were living "some all together, and others in sheds or dugouts" on the hillsides between Sopris Canyon and Jerryville. *Photo courtesy of Steelworks Center of the West, Bessemer Historical Society, Pueblo, Colorado.*

The houses at each coal camp were owned by the mining companies, and employees were allowed to rent them as long as they were working for that mine. The Sociology Department of CF&I published monthly periodicals/news journals that included articles on home beautification, and it also held contests that motivated the residents to maintain well-cared-for homes and yards. Each year, CF&I awarded cash prizes for the most attractive home, best yard and best garden. *Photo courtesy of Steelworks Center of the West, Bessemer Historical Society, Pueblo, Colorado.*

The second Sopris school was built in 1890, at the mouth of the canyon, across from what became the location of the YMCA but a bit to the north. The population of Sopris was at 1,600 by 1904 and increased to 1,700 between 1910 and 1912 before beginning a decline.[33] When the 1913–14 strike was over and progress was being made in improving the working conditions and earnings of the miners, the young men who had come to work in the mines prior to the strike began to marry the daughters of coworkers and begin families. Those who came as families with one or two children often added more to their families, and by the time the census was conducted in 1920, 35 percent of the residents in all Sopris neighborhoods were between zero and ten years of age. The next-largest age group was between twenty-one and forty, and 18 percent of residents were between eleven and twenty years old. These growing families created a need to expand the school to include grades seven and eight, which it did in 1916, and plans began for an even larger school. The second school served the community for a couple more years.

Room to grow! With the rising demand for steel and the rapid immigration of workers, the small adobe school that had served the community was replaced by this two-story building at the corner of Wolcott and Dexter. It eventually added grades seven and eight in 1916 and served the town from approximately 1901 through 1918, when the "new" and final school was built at Dexter and James. *Photo courtesy of Steelworks Center of the West, Bessemer Historical Society, Pueblo, Colorado.*

The third and last Sopris school opened in 1918, across from the Colorado Supply Company Store. As the mines lost the ability to pay in company scrip and other merchants entered the neighborhoods to provide for the miners' needs, the Colorado Supply Company stores closed down and disappeared from the camps, in this case leaving a large open area that was filled by the new gymnasium in the first half of the 1950s. *Photo courtesy of Faoro Family Photo Archives.*

The largest and last school was constructed on the southeast corner of Dexter Street where it intersected James Avenue, just across from the Colorado Supply Company Store. It was dedicated in 1918, with a celebration that lasted from March 19 through March 23. People began to relocate from the canyon homes to live in the Sopris neighborhoods, allowing them to be nearer this school and the Dexter Street businesses.

In the 1920s, some of the mines began to close due to a shift in the demand for coal and after the explosion of 1922 at the Sopris mine. Miners began to commute to other nearby mines while continuing to live in the Sopris neighborhoods and send their children to Lincoln School.

Chapter 3

ST. THOMAS

T he Denver Fuel Company was incorporated on September 9, 1887, with the objectives of the organization being

to acquire, purchase, own, hold, work, lease, and sell coal lands and other lands in the State of Colorado and elsewhere; to prospect for, develop, mine and sell coal and other minerals; to deal in coal and all kinds of fuel, natural and manufactured; to manufacture coke and other artificial articles; to purchase, construct, acquire and operate all machinery and apparatus for mining and manufacturing as aforesaid, including the construction and operation of rail and trainways for the mining and moving of coal and other materials, with all necessary side tracks, and the building and leasing of houses to be used by miners…and others; and in general to do any and all the aforesaid and such other things as may promote the general purposes of such corporation, or may be necessary or proper in the successful transaction of its business.

The document was signed by J.C. Osgood, Samuel N. Wood and Henry R. Wolcott and notarized by Henry F. Jolly.[34]

May 12, 1888, at 4:00 p.m. marks the beginning of the town of St. Thomas, as recorded by Eugenio Garcia, deputy recorder, acting on behalf of Jesus Maria Garcia, recorder (see Appendix A, "Plat Filings"). Thomas Martin purchased eighty acres in Sections 27 and 28, and with George W. Thompson—president of the Raton Coal & Coke Company, which was located at Thompson on the Long's Cañon branch of the Denver-Texas & Ft. Worth Railroad (D.T. & F.W. RR)—he

> *laid out and Sub-divided into lots and blocks to be known as "St. Thomas"*
> *a certain tract of land, as shown by the annexed plat, and situated in the*
> *S ½ of SE ¼ Section 28 Township 33 S. R 64 W, in Las Animas*
> *County, State of Colorado, and the Streets and alleys as shown by said plat*
> *are dedicated to public use. In part, the community that would house the*
> *miners to be employed by the Denver Fuel Company, and to encourage the*
> *development of businesses the people would need. The 1888 Polk's City*
> *Directory indicates that three general merchandise stores, a lumber yard,*
> *a furniture store, a butcher, a baker, and a barber—plus four saloons—*
> *were part of the town at the time it was printed. Two saloons also offered*
> *lodging, one as a hotel and the other as a boarding house. In addition to*
> *lodging and drinking, one included a billiards hall.*[35]

Of St. Thomas, *Polk's Trinidad (Colorado) City Directory, Volume 1888* states:

> *It is situated in the very center of the coal mines of Southern Colorado and*
> *on the Las Animas River, which affords an inexhaustible supply of pure*
> *mountain water. It is on the line of the gateway of the Rocky Mountains*
> *and near the pass over the celebrated Raton Peak....The growth of the*
> *place since it was laid out last spring has been phenomenal and if the*
> *same enterprise characterizes its founders in the future it will continue to*
> *grow. The Denver Fuel Company's mines adjoining St. Thomas gives this*
> *point stability.*

As predicted, St. Thomas continued to be a desirable place to live, with its neighborhood school for children in kindergarten through grade eight, its church and more businesses (and saloons) than any other neighborhood. It was the largest among the neighborhoods, covering twenty-five blocks (approximately equal to Main Sopris and Ferrelville/Jerryville combined).

The St. Thomas church was established on lots 20 through 24 in block 12, deeded to Father Charles M. Pinto by Thomas Martin on May 16, 1890. By 1911, it was one of thirty-two mission churches in the coal camps.[36] Adjacent to St. Thomas Church was St. Thomas School, but it was not a parochial school, as the name might suggest. The initial intent was that the younger students not living in Main Sopris would attend St. Thomas School and then transfer to the high school. Parents didn't always make that choice,

Above: Saint Thomas Church was built on lots deeded to Father Charles M. Pinto in 1890 by Thomas Martin, a founder of the St. Thomas neighborhood. Priests were serving many parishes, so at times the church had Mass only once each month, and annual sacramental events like First Holy Communion had to fit into that schedule. These cousins, Patti Sebben (daughter of Adolph and Mary Ida [Terry] Sebben) and Beverly Sebben (daughter of Joe and Minnie [Machone] Sebben), received the sacrament from Father Flynn, assisted by altar boy George Zanotelli. *Photo courtesy of Sebben Family Photo Archives.*

Opposite: May 28, 1938, is when this photo of the young children of Sopris was taken. For some, it marked their first communion, and for others, it was part of the celebration of the Virgin Mary. It includes children up to the eighth grade, some of whom attended St. Thomas School and others who attended Lincoln School in Main Sopris. An annual high school baccalaureate Mass was celebrated at the church as well. *Photo courtesy of Faoro Family Photo Archives.*

and as with the children of Sopris Plaza, for a small tuition fee, children from St. Thomas, Jerryville and Piedmont could attend Lincoln School from kindergarten through high school.

LIFE AFTER THE MINES

The Denver Fuel Company's involvement with St. Thomas was rather short-lived, from filing incorporation papers in September 1887 to building the first one hundred coke ovens in May 1888—ovens that would also be used by Colorado Coal and Iron[37]—to selling the mine to the Colorado Fuel Company in February 1889.[38] In January 1888, the mine was filling fifty train cars each day, and it was anticipated that the output would continue to increase. The St. Thomas Mine appears in the 1887–88 biennial state mining inspector's report, and the makeup of the land—the width of the coal veins and the percentage of rock and silt—is included in three drawings of the stratification of the land. Of the mine, the report states:

> *For new mines* [they] *have shipped a remarkable amount of coal in a short space of time....The coal seam is about seven feet in thickness, is comparatively clean and of fine coking quality. The roof is composed of arenaceous slate, and the floor of dark shale....*

The plant of this company, in all its details, is modern, and is so constructed as to insure a large output....

Much credit is due to Mr. J.A. Kebler, the company's general manager, for the rapidity and manner in which he opened these mines, and worked them up to an output of 1,000 tons per day, and for the completeness of all other improvements in detail there.[39]

In February 1889, the Denver Fuel Company mines were sold to the Colorado Fuel Company for half a million dollars, and then they, in turn, became part of the October 1892 merger of the Colorado Fuel Company and the Colorado Coal and Iron Company that created the Colorado Fuel and Iron Corporation.[40]

Perfect timing! The Mondragon home, located across from St. Thomas Church, was begun by Ted Langowski, even though rumors of the dam coming in the near future were rampant. While Ted was building the house, the Mondragon family was in the Denver area because of a shortage of work in Las Animas County. Twists of fate brought the Mondragon family back to Sopris and sent Ted and his family north, but not before he sold his not-quite-complete house to the Mondragon family, who added their own finishing touches. As a result, Paul was able to complete his education in Sopris and graduate with his childhood friends in 1965—the last class to graduate from Lincoln High School. *Photo courtesy of Paul Mondragon Photo Archives.*

The 1910 census recorded 24 families residing in St. Thomas, and by 1940, that number had risen to over 120. Many men still worked in the mines, now traveling to Valdez or other nearby mines since local mines were no longer operating, but the 1940 census indicates that more men were employed through the WPA on road work, construction and waterworks projects than worked for the mines.[41] As people left the company houses established by the Denver Fuel Company, others became owners of the homes. Additional homes were constructed.

As years passed, saloons continued to be the most popular businesses in St. Thomas, and it seems that everyone owned a saloon for at least a short period of time. Between 1910 and 1925, city directories listed over ten saloons in the Sopris neighborhoods, most of which were in St. Thomas.

TAVERN OWNERS ACROSS THE YEARS
AS LISTED IN THE POLK'S CITY DIRECTORIES

1892   Bianchi and Co.
Bonfadini, L.
GardGaro, D.
McGuane and Plummer
Valentine and Vvegher

1901   Bianchi, John
Bonfadini, Leo
Carli, Angelo
Shaw, George

1904   Bargoni, Thomas
Bianchi, John—bartender Borgo, John
Bonfadini, Leon
Bryacich, Casamero
Carli, Angelo (saloon and bakery)
Dawe, Robert J.
Matta, Charles—bartender Shaw, George
Menapace, Paul
Orekar, John
Schimenz, August—bartender Dawe, R.J.
Shaw, George

1905   Bergamo, Thomas
Bianchi, Teresa
Bonfadini, Joseph
Bryacich, Casamero
Carli, Angelo (saloon and bakery)
Unek, John

1907   Bergamo, Thomas
Bianchi, Teresa
Bonfadini, Joseph
Bryacich, Casamero
Carli, Angelo (saloon and bakery)
Mosele, Peter (fine wines, liquor, cigars)
Unek, John

1909   Bergamo, Thomas
Bianchi, Teresa
Bonfadini, Joseph
Bryacich, Casamero
Carli, Angelo (saloon and bakery)
Chambers, Edward
Mosele, Peter (fine wines, liquor, cigars)
Unek, John

1910   Bergamo, Thomas
Bocacio, Tony
Bonato, Joe
Bonfadini, Bert
Brunelli, Frank
Carli, Angelo (fine wines, liquors and cigars, bakery)
Chambers, Edward—American Saloon
Dambrosio, Jasper
Oneratti, Coletto
Reiter, Frank
Serano, Valdayo

1912   American Saloon—Edward Chambers
Bonato, Joe
Butero, Jasper

Copeland, Neil—Sopris hotel, new theater, saloon
Dambrosio, Jasper
Garenzini, Enrico—saloon and boarding
Gaudino and Mundich
Luccia, Joe
Oneratti, Colleto
Raye, Charles H. (son-in-law of Bianchi)
Reiter, Frank
Rocco, Tony
Ubertti, Otti, and Viecellio, Anton—bakery and saloon
Verdaglo, B.

1915   Bonato, Joe
Butero, Jasper
Butero, Sebastiano
Dambrosio, Jasper
Guadino and Mundich
Luccia, Joseph—saloon and general store
Oneratti, Coletto
Rocco, Tony
Uberti and Bonato (Otti Uberti and J.D. Bonato)—bakery and saloon
Verdaglo, Anton
Viecellio, Anton

1918   Bonato, Joseph—soft drinks
Rocco, Tony—soft drinks
Verdaglo, Anton—soft drinks
14 soft drinks venues in directory

1921   No soft drinks listed

1924   No soft drinks in Sopris; two confectionery shops, Rocco and Verdalgo

With Prohibition, the number of taverns and saloons decreased, and some found other trades. A greater number of grocers opened in those years, and Tony Rocco and Anton Verdaglo opened confectionery shops. Opaque milk bottles were opaque for a reason.

In 1918, when Prohibition was the law, there are no saloons listed in the city directory, and Joe Bonato, Tony Rocco and Anton Verdaglo are listed as soft drink retailers. While that may be the public record, Chuck Cambruzzi says his father had a talent for making whiskey that he distributed at the mine with the knowledge of the management,[42] and the Baca family recounts having access to tunnels under the roads from the store their grandfather Roy Baca bought from Antonio and Cruccia Martorana. Charles Martorano[43] clarified that the store was rented out prior to being sold to Roy Baca, and when his uncle went to collect the rent, the person who greeted him at the door politely cautioned him that it was very dangerous for him to be there and it would be best for him to remain at home and let them bring the rent to him.[44]

In the end, three St. Thomas saloons remained—Angelo Brunelli's Frontier Tavern, Dona's Silver Dollar and the DeAngelis brothers' Big Six. The taverns were frequented by the miners and members of the community, but they were more than drinking establishments. Family members and

If the walls could talk! Emma Vigil Baca (holding Anthony Baca) and Nina Baca Santillanes (holding Luis Santillanes) visit Juan Rosendo "Roy" and Venina Baca, the babies' grandparents. The store was originally owned by Antonio and Cruccia Martorana, then leased during Prohibition and prior to the Baca family buying the store. Tunnels beneath the store and street suggest that moonshine may have moved through them. *Photo courtesy of Joseph Anthony Baca and Baca Family Photo Archives.*

The Frontier Tavern, owned by Angelo and Teresa Brunelli, was one of several taverns located in St. Thomas amid the neighboring houses. It was a scheduled stop after a day of mining for many in the area, including the Martorano brothers, who worked at their family's mine in Riley Canyon. Stories are told about how each brother had his own mug that was well preserved on "his" shelf, where he could easily locate it each night for a beer after work. The tavern was a popular place for many in the neighborhood, and the door was seldom blocked by deep snow. *Photo courtesy of Brunelli Family Photo Archives.*

friends of all ages were welcome, as Lois Terry Mantelli remembers. She and Irene DeAngelis, daughter of the owner, spent their afternoons sitting in a booth at the back, doing their homework.[45] Taverns were also where people came together for special and significant times, such as a final gathering before reporting for duty in World War II.

The second most common privately owned businesses were the neighborhood stores, and here, again, St. Thomas had more than most. The Bianchi store was one of the oldest, established by John Bianchi in 1874. His wife came to the United States in 1891 with their adopted daughter, Rose. John passed away prior to 1910, leaving Teresa and Rose to run the store with the help of Rose's husband, Charles Raye.

The new Brunelli store was next door to the Bianchi general merchandise store and saloon. The night of August 1, 1924, saw a little excitement when fire broke out in the Bianchi store and high winds carried the flames to the

Above: As troops were called up for World War II, these men from St. Thomas gathered one last time at the Frontier Tavern before some of them reported for enlistment in 1942. *Left to right*: Frank Archuleta, William Zanotelli, Tony Battistone, Paul Butero, Erminio DeAngelis, Sam Butero (*holding hat*), Orazio Battistone (*with bottle in hand*). *Photo courtesy of JoAnn Battistone LePlatte and Battistone Family Photo Archives.*

Opposite: The new Brunelli Store was built in St. Thomas by Frank Brunelli, Sam and Angelo's father, after the old store was sold to J.B. and Marie Cunico. In addition to offering grocery items, it was the Sopris post office, and Mary Brunelli was the postmaster. The Brunellis' son and daughter, Kenneth and Konnie, helped in the store and attended Trinidad State Junior College before leaving a vacancy that was filled by other youth of the community, including Chuck Cambruzzi and Lois Terry Mantelli. *Photo courtesy of Brunelli Family Photo Archives.*

Brunelli store. Neighbors responded and were able to remove items from the living quarters, but merchandise worth an estimated $10,000 was lost to the fire—though covered by insurance.[46] Both stores were rebuilt, and the Brunelli store continued to be the Sopris Post Office as well.

Louis Rocco ran a pool hall known as Spook's that served pop and snack items to the local youth. Those who frequented Spook's spoke of a back room where their dads would gather to play cards or barbotte—not high-stakes gambling but a way to pass the time and enjoy good company.

Trapper Falagrady owned a barbershop that served not only St. Thomas but also many men and boys in the Sopris neighborhoods.

GOING DOWN TO THE RIVER TO PLAY

Few of those who grew up in St. Thomas can say they never ventured into the shallow waters of the Purgatoire on a hot summer day. With age comes wisdom, but floods were seldom and unpredictable, so parents' and grandparents' warnings went unheeded until the youth witnessed them for themselves. One remembers enjoying summer days in the river with neighborhood friends until a mom invariably became aware and came out to yell at them to get out and assure them their mothers would hear about their choices.[47] For the young of St. Thomas, the river was their Neverland, or their Mississippi River, where captured chickens could be plucked, cleaned and deep-fried in a no. 3 coffee can of boiling oil heated over a campfire.[48]

With no early warning system and a river that took on water during summer rains in the cooler mountains, there were no alerts to let townsfolk know the river was flooding. One resident vividly recalls, as a girl, crossing the shallow riverbed with friends to sit on the opposite bank and play— when, suddenly, they heard an unfamiliar sound and the air was filled with a malodorous stench. Catching a glimpse of tree limbs and water around the bend and moving toward them, they made a mad dash for the St. Thomas side of the river and headed to high ground just as the wall of water filled with debris raced down the riverbed that had been so shallow just minutes ago. They were safely across and had run an estimated twenty feet up the hillside, yet the spray from the raging river reached their feet as it rushed by. Seeing was believing.[49]

Chapter 4

MAIN SOPRIS

THE EARLY YEARS

Although a bit of a sleepy little town, Sopris had a colorful history that included ties to many of the United States' most well-known industrialists—Gates, Gould and Rockefeller.

When the Sopris mine opened in 1886, company housing was extremely limited, so workers were allowed to rent a bit of land and construct their own homes nearby until company houses were constructed. Company buildings surrounded the mine: the mule stable, the washery, the tipple and the offices.

The demand for coal was closely linked to the demand for the steel rails necessary for the advancement of the United States' railroad industry. The railroad was more than just a way to move people, commodities and freight; it was how men became wealthy and how they lost fortunes. During the Gilded Age, between 1870 and 1890, the race to connect the railroads of the East to those coming from the West was a high-stakes competition with a few key players. General William Jackson Palmer was one of those men, establishing the Pueblo Steel Mill in the late 1800s. Between 1880 and 1890, 70,400 miles of track were laid, bringing the national total from 93,200 to 163,600 miles, with the greatest increase in the western states, and the management of the Pueblo steel mill signed a contract for 30,000 tons of steel rails in August 1882. It produced 125 tons per day to meet the order.[50]

Mules were used to haul the small, loaded coal cars from the mine to the tipple, where the coal was sorted and train cars were filled. Each mine had at least one mule barn and a corral adjacent to the mine where nonworking mules were kept as they recovered from illness or injury, or when they needed new shoes, but the working mules were housed underground, where their eyes became used to the dark. A mine might have between one hundred and two hundred mules, which were purchased for between $150 and $300 each. Mines employed men who worked as the stable boss and as rope riders and drivers to work with the mules. *Photo courtesy of Steelworks Center of the West, Bessemer Historical Society, Pueblo, Colorado.*

Steel production required coal, and many mines in Las Animas County produced a high-grade coking coal, positioning Las Animas County as the county that produced more high-grade coking coal than any other county in Colorado.[51] By 1888, there was talk of constructing a second steel mill closer to the mines just outside of El Moro:

> *The News reporter was informed by reliable authority to-day that the Colorado Coal and Iron company have issued orders to have work commence immediately on the artesian well—now down about 400 feet—in the town of El Moro....Fifty thousand stakes have also been placed on the large tract of land northwest of the town, and in a few days a corps of surveyors will be at work platting the ground into town lots. This company, for the past two months, has been doing some quiet but effectual work, and it is*

now a decided fact that it will locate a steel plant in that vicinity or nearer Trinidad, on a much larger scale than the company's plant now in operation in Pueblo. A large smelter is also talked of by the same company.[52]

To meet the needs of the miners' households, the Colorado Supply Company was incorporated on August 22, 1888, and opened its first store at Sopris on September 1, 1888, at what would become the northeast corner of Dexter Street and James Avenue (see map in Appendix A).[53] The original stockholders of the company were men often associated with the area mines, including John Cleveland Osgood, J.A. Kebler, D.C. Beaman, E.G. Tisdale, D. Sullivan and S.N. Wood.[54]

On February 20, 1889, the Denver Fuel Company established the streets and alleys that became known as Main Sopris. The document was signed by W.H. James, vice president of the company.[55] Unlike the streets of St. Thomas, which are named after presidents, the streets of Main Sopris are

Early Sopris began to the west of Sopris Canyon and was built in proximity to the Colorado Supply Company Store, the two-story building to the left of center in this photo. The Colorado Supply Company was incorporated in August 1888, and the Sopris store was the first of the company's stores to open, the very next month. The third Sopris school was eventually built on the south side of Dexter Street, directly across from the store, and when the store eventually closed and was torn down, the large area was a perfect location for a new school gymnasium. *Photo courtesy of Steelworks Center of the West, Bessemer Historical Society, Pueblo, Colorado.*

named for the board of directors of the Denver Fuel Company, as noted in a *Rocky Mountain News* article from February 25, 1889, which states:

> *Among the stockholders are the following well-known men: Dennis Sullivan, S.M. Wood, Edward O. Wolcott, Henry R. Wolcott, Henry M. Porter, J.B. Dexter, James B. Grant, Edward Eddy and W.H. James.*[56]

In February 1889, the Denver Fuel Company sold the Sopris mines to the Colorado Fuel Company, and within a few years, the mines became part of the merger between that company and Colorado Coal and Iron (plus additional lands), becoming holdings of the Colorado Fuel and Iron Company.[57] The mines continued under the leadership of John C. Osgood, Julian T. Kebler, Alfred C. Cass and John L. Jerome until 1903, when John D. Rockefeller and his associate, George G. Gould, were able to gain controlling interest in the company, thus providing the fuel source for manufacturing the rails they needed to support their railroad interests.[58] It was announced on June 25, 1903, that

> *John D. Rockefeller has bought the Colorado Fuel & Iron company and has harmonized the differences of the several factions battling for its control…. Mr. Rockefeller's policy is to build up this Western railroad and he shall keep the Minnequa furnaces going. This means continued prosperity for Pueblo. Mr. Osgood has resigned as chairman of the board.*[59]

Battling the East Coast robber barons for control of the company that they created and built up took a toll on the physical and mental health of the four founders, and they came out of it having lost significant fortunes.[60] In the end, Osgood, as it turned out, had done much that allowed Rockefeller and Gould to gain major interest due to a need for capital to complete upgrades and improvements for which he had underestimated the total amount required.[61] He wanted to add more capacity to the steel mill and found he did not have sufficient funds to complete the project without additional revenue. Perhaps he issued more shares of stock to raise the necessary funds and all those new shares were picked up by Rockefeller and Gould. In any case, they now owned more than 50 percent of the company's stock and had controlling interest. Kebler, Cass and Jerome had placed their trust in Chairman Osgood's ability to protect their interests. When it became apparent that it had been misplaced, they united to prepare a suit to recover what they had lost—but the suit was never filed as, one by one, their lives came to an abrupt or unanticipated end. Cass died suddenly on July 4; Kebler was found deceased in his home on November 20; and Jerome did not awaken on November 26—his death was attributed to having taken too much of a sleeping aid he had turned to during these troubling times. The Gilded Age was coming to an end, but the ambitions that drove it and the rails that carried it stretched far from the financial center of New York and into the cities and coal camps of Southern Colorado.

As the wrangling for control of the CF&I took place over a period of years, miners throughout Colorado were on strike in various districts from 1901 through 1904, seeking an eight-hour day, a 2,000-pound ton instead of a 2,400-pound ton, a checking man of their choice, a paycheck every two weeks instead of only at the end of each month, a 20 percent increase in pay and the abolishment of the scrip system.[62] It is believed that from these early years, Rockefeller used these strikes as an excuse to shut down the steel mill, thus casting the blame on the strikers for putting others out of work, even though the reality was that the mill could have remained open. The groundwork was being laid to turn others against the mine workers, during the present strike and in the future.[63] By March 1904, Governor Peabody had declared Las Animas County to be in a state of rebellion and insurrection, based on statements made by the local authorities, and the state's militia was sent to "quell the insurrection."[64]

Nine years later (1913), the miners were still striking for improved working conditions that closely reflected the goals of the 1904 strike. They wanted:

- The United Mine Workers of America to be recognized as their representatives to be negotiated with regarding labor issues.
- A 10 percent increase in wages on the tonnage rates.[65]
- An eight-hour workday—something that had been achieved a few years earlier by the striking garment workers of the Triangle Shirtwaist Factory.
- Payment for "dead work"—time spent stabilizing the tunnels where the coal was being mined by adding roof supports and laying track for the mining cars to travel on.
- The right to elect their own checkweighmen, the men who determined how much coal they had loaded (believing that the company men were cheating them and recording a lesser amount).
- To choose their own boarding places.

- To select their own doctor, rather than being required to use the company doctor assigned to each camp.
- The Colorado mining laws to be enforced equitably at all mines and an end to the company guard system.[66]

The abolishment of payment to miners in company scrip preceded the strike, but incidents of attempting to continue the practice were well known.

In September 1913, a strike was called, and the mine owners responded as they had previously, during the strike of 1901 through 1904: by refusing to recognize the union and refusing to meet with the miners' representatives, bringing in armed guards instead. As the conflict grew, Governor Ammons ordered over one thousand members of the state's militia to the area. The strike became violent; both sides took up weapons, and some union advocates used their skills—and the dynamite they had originally purchased for work—to blow up bridges and buildings belonging to the mine owners.

On Sunday, April 20, 1914, the tent colony at Ludlow, in Las Animas County, was set ablaze. When the smoke cleared and the damage was assessed, the bodies of two women and eleven children were found in a "cellar" that had been excavated under a tent to provide safety and warmth from the bitter cold winds. The world watched in horror and dismay, and although the striking workers were not successful in having their demands met, after outcries and the insistence of leaders including Governor Ammons and President Wilson, the strike ended in December 1914.

The Federal Industrial Relations Commission began an investigation into the underlying causes of the Colorado coal strike, and the first witnesses were Governor Ammons and governor-elect Carlson. Other witnesses included, but were not limited to, John D. Rockefeller Jr., the head of CF&I; J.F. Welborn, president of the Colorado Fuel and Iron Company; John C. Osgood, chairman of the board of directors of the Victor-American Fuel Company; David W. Brown, president of the Rocky Mountain Fuel Company; E.V. Brake, state commissioner of labor; John McLennan, president of United Mine Workers of America, District No. 15; and Frank J. Hayes, vice president of the United Mine Workers of America.[67]

In the eyes of most Americans, the Rockefeller family was profit oriented, without regard for those doing the work that allowed them their wealth. Reports were generated to clearly define the conditions in the coal camps, and with so many thinking him an out-of-touch owner, John D. Rockefeller Jr. came to the coalfields of Southern Colorado to see for himself and to let these people get to know him. He arrived in September 1915 with an

He called at the little adobe shack of Joe Mazarise, who had worked at Sopris for a period of seventeen years and raised a family of seventeen children. He made himself solid with the Italian and his wife instantly when he picked up the couple's smallest child and fondled it.

"Mr. Rockefeller is a might fine man," declared the proud mother after her visitor had departed.

"He likes children; that always means a good man."

The often-violent strike of 1913–14 was in newspapers across the United States and in Europe, and when two women and eleven children died at the Ludlow tent camp, absent owner of the Colorado Fuel and Iron Company John D. Rockefeller Jr. was a monster in many eyes. It was obvious to him that he needed to change his image, so he hired Ivy Lee as his publicist and William Lyon Mackenzie King as his labor relations advisor. In September 1915, the three visited the Colorado coal camps that Rockefeller owned, after Ivy Lee had come to Colorado on two previous trips to get to know the area and establish contacts among the local CF&I managers, who helped him envision the best way to improve Rockefeller's image. While in Colorado, Rockefeller visited families in the camps, had lunch at the miners' boardinghouse and visited some of the miners' private homes, as described in a news article published in the *Salt Lake Telegram*. *Photo from "Rockefeller Sleeps in Cabin Simplicity of Magnate Pleases," Salt Lake Telegram, September 25, 1915.*

entourage that included Ivy Lee, the public relations coordinator who had already made two trips to Colorado to assess the situation and figure out the most effective ways to gain the support of the miners and their families and the public at large, and W.L. Mackenzie King (Canada's minister of labour from 1909 to 1911), who had become part of the Rockefeller Foundation in October 1914 as a labor relations consultant.[68] While in Colorado, he went to great lengths to "walk in [the miners'] shoes" and dress in their clothing. He visited each camp and focused on spending time among the miners and their families, dancing with the wives and daughters of the miners at Cameron and stopping by the home of Joe and Carmela Mazzarise in Sopris. (The Mazzarise family arrived in Colorado between 1900 and 1901, and seven children lived in the home to adulthood—instead of the seventeen reported in the papers.)

What Rockefeller saw was a need to provide these people with better homes and a community center affiliated with the YMCA organization that would include a reading room, space for classes, a gymnasium and a space where youth, families and the community could gather. The YMCA Clubhouse was built on Wolcott Street, at the mouth of Sopris Canyon, after John D. Rockefeller Jr.'s visit in 1915; it served as the gymnasium, library/reading room and dance hall for the area until 1954, when the new gymnasium was ready for use. A "cottage" dedicated to the young children was just being completed (and was dedicated on October 15, 1915), and Rockefeller promised a band shell where the community could gather to listen to the camp band. By 1916, much had been achieved.

After visiting his mining camps in Las Animas County, John D. Rockefeller Jr. saw the need for a YMCA community center at each camp. The Sopris "Clubhouse" was on Wolcott Avenue, just south of the school and near the Sopris Canyon entrance. It included a bowling alley and was where the basketball teams competed, school dances were held, classes for area women took place and impromptu "sock hops" occurred after school as long as Mr. Zancanaro was willing to oversee them, according to Bernie Morgan, who graduated with Marlene Zancanaro. *Photo courtesy of Steelworks Center of the West, Bessemer Historical Society, Pueblo, Colorado.*

With the strike behind them, the young immigrants continued to marry, and a new generation of Americans filled the community and journeyed together as they navigated the Old Country cultures, values and beliefs of their parents and grandparents while taking part in new experiences and new opportunities in this new culture. Many of the fathers and grandfathers worked in the mines, while the mothers and grandmothers remained in the home raising the children, but over time, there were those who chose new paths and became small-business owners.

Looking west from the corner of Wolcott Avenue and Dexter Street (essentially, looking down the "Main Street" of Main Sopris), you would have seen the grocery and general stores, the beauty and barbershop, the school and gymnasium and small in-house businesses that were found to the south along James Avenue (see the plat map in Appendix A). The Sam Colletti Mercantile Store was the first business in Main Sopris, on the south side of Dexter on land acquired from Jonathan Reinoehls on October 11, 1906. Across the street was the Reinoehls/Salvatore/Sebben general store and cobbler shop, midway on that side of the block. Crossing Eddy Avenue, the Furia Beauty and Barber Shop was on the northwest corner, and at the corner of James Avenue and Dexter Street was the DeAngelis home and dairy. With no lush pastureland to graze, the DeAngelis cows were allowed to roam the town, foraging along the streets and alleys, in undeveloped parcels, down at the baseball field and in unfenced yards and gardens. As one resident remembers, they would sometimes get into gardens and "leave fertilizer behind."[69] That fertilizer, those cow pies, sometimes appeared on the playground or near the school, and Nick Furia, class of '47, remembers that his friend Corky would sometimes collect a dry one and sneak it into class to place on a girl's chair where she would sit on it unknowingly.[70] Continuing west beyond James Avenue on Dexter Street was Bruno Faldutto's family and his small meat-processing business, which supplied beef to area stores.[71]

If you turned left on James Avenue and headed south, toward LHS, you'd see August Zamborelli's shop, where he did welding and other trades. Continuing south across Sullivan Street, you'd find the Cerame home and Frank's eighteen-wheeler. Frank's parents, Anna and John, lived on the back side of the block on Wood Street. Anna was a teacher and knew English, so she was often called on to help as an interpreter when new people came to the United States and needed assistance communicating. Lena and Virginio Fantin lived next door and raised four children. Virginio gave private music lessons and was the band instructor for the school. Many from Sopris have him to thank for their early music instruction.

Above: The 1950s saw several changes in Sopris as the demand for coal declined and families began to leave the community, but there was still a need for goods and services for those remaining. One main road connected Main Sopris to Highway 12 at the west near Sopris Plaza and to the east across the Blasi Bridge, and from the corner of Wolcott Avenue and Dexter Street, it was possible to see most of the businesses. There was one active store, a beauty and barbershop and the school and gymnasium. Other businesses were home-based. May 29, 1959, was the centennial celebration of the 1859 "Rush to the Rockies" that began with the discovery of gold near Pikes Peak, so Western wear was the style of the day. *Photo courtesy of Faoro Family Photo Archives.*

Opposite, bottom: The first store in Main Sopris to compete with the Colorado Supply Company Store was built on the north side of Dexter Street, just a block away from the Colorado Supply Company Store (behind children). It was initially owned by Jonathan Reinoehls, and a listing for the store in *Polk's Trinidad Colorado City Directory Volume 1909* advertises that the store was a source for "drugs, hardware, dry goods, notions, cigars, soda fountain, etc." and that Mr. Reinoehls was an agent for Victor Safe Co. and a notary public. The store was sold to Pete Salvatore in the early 1920s (possibly after Jonathan's death in 1924), and he and his wife, Jane, raised their children there. Many remember the kindness of the Salvatore family, including Bernie Morgan, who recalls them giving out penny candy to the schoolchildren on their lunch break. The Salvatore family sold the store to its final owners, Adolph and Mary Ida Sebben, in 1953, and the Sebben family ran it until 1970. Mary Ida became the postmaster after Mary Brunelli relocated. *Photo courtesy of Faoro Family Photo Archives.*

Competing for a piece of the miners' market, Sam Colletti opened a grocery and general merchandise store in the early 1900s at the corner of Dexter Street and Eddy Avenue—across the street and one block east of the Colorado Supply Company Store. Adjacent to the store, on the east side, was the residence where Sam (Saverio) and Mary Ida raised their six children, Mary, Joseph, Anna, Rosie, Michael and Samuel. Mary, Anna and Rosie married locally and became Mrs. Lawrence Terry, Mrs. Charles Dintelman and Mrs. Jim Buccola. *Photo courtesy of Faoro Family Photo Archives.*

The Furia beauty and barbershop remained a part of Sopris until the end, with daughters Theresa and Rose becoming beauticians and son Nick becoming a barber. The shop (*far left*) was adjacent to the Furia home on Dexter Street across from the school grounds, and Theresa operated it as a beauty shop Monday through Friday, while Nick welcomed customers on some evenings and Saturday mornings when he wasn't teaching at Trinidad State Junior College. Rose married and lived in Trinidad, where she owned and operated Rose's Beauty Salon. *Photo courtesy of Faoro Family Photo Archives.*

The Methodist Episcopal church was tucked into a neighborhood at the corner of Wolcott Avenue and Wood Street. Much of the community was of European descent and thereby of the Catholic faith, worshiping at St. Thomas Church in the St. Thomas neighborhood, but a few came to worship at the Methodist Episcopal Church as well. It is first mentioned in the 1901 Trinidad city directory.

By far the largest employer of local residents was the public school system. It attracted people from beyond Sopris and often included alumni who had been inspired by a teacher who had returned to Sopris to teach—showing them that they, too, could be influential in the lives of those slightly younger than themselves. In the mid-1950s, the school district purchased small homes for faculty members and placed them on the school district property that had been the site of the second school.

In the 1920s and 1930s, teachers and staff for the vocational programs such as woodworking and fabrication, the school band and noninstructional

Top: Fresh milk! When the depression hit the coal industry, many families from Sopris had to seek employment elsewhere, so the DeAngelis family moved to Michigan. The 1940 census found them back in Sopris; Rocco was once again working in the mines, along with his sons Louis and Angelo. Domenica began a local dairy business, with a few cows that grazed in the neighborhoods each day, providing fresh milk for customers each morning. *Photo courtesy of DeAngelis & Zamborelli Family Photo Archives.*

Bottom: Irene and Frank Cerame stand by his Diamond T truck, parked beside their home, about as far east as you could go on James Street. As the town had only one paved street and narrow alleys throughout, Frank was fortunate to have little traffic to contend with when returning home with his semi. While he was gone, Irene not only kept the home fires burning, but she also kept the stovetop hot. She was known for her amazing popcorn balls, candy apples and much more. *Photo courtesy of Cerame Family Photo Archives.*

Top: Anna and John Cerame and their young daughter, Seraphina, came to the United States from Cefalu, on the northern coast of Sicily, at the beginning of the twentieth century, first residing in Louisiana and then making their way to Sopris, where John began to work in the mines. In this photo, they are with their granddaughter Bernadine, daughter of their youngest son, Frank. *Photo courtesy of Cerame Family Photo Archive.*

Bottom: Virginio Fantin with sons Louis and Paul. Virginio Fantin came to the United States from Arsiè, Italy, in the province of Belluno to work in the mines. A talented musician, he immediately became involved with the town band and became a friend to bandleader Paul Costa. Spending time with Paul and his family, Virginio became acquainted with Paul's daughter Lena. They married and raised a family of two daughters and two sons. *Photo courtesy of Ruth Berry Wilson and Fantin Family Photo Archives.*

Neither steeple nor bells called attention to the Methodist Episcopal church that was tucked away along Wolcott Avenue across from the YMCA Clubhouse (*center, background*). Because Sopris was dominantly made up of immigrants from Europe—Italy, Austria, the Tyrol region—and Mexico, most families attended the Roman Catholic church in St. Thomas, but not all. *Photo courtesy of Faoro Family Photo Archives.*

A bit more diversity was added to the Lincoln School faculty as the years went on, with new hires complementing the alumni faculty members. *Front row, left to right*: Teresa McGinn, Mrs. Langowski, Mrs. Pachelli. *Middle row, left to right*: Gene McGinn, Ralph Fausone, Ms. Gagliardi, Estella Faoro. *Back row, left to right*: Martin Anzelini, Anthony Faoro, Mr. Sphar. Because of the strong connection between Sopris High School and Trinidad Junior College, most teachers graduating in the 1940s began their training at TJC, so many of these colleagues had been friends for years. *Photo courtesy of sopriscoloradoreborn.com.*

Above: Another one returns, and a cornhusker joins! By December 1953, John Sebben Jr. had returned to Sopris as a social studies teacher, and Murray Francescato, from Nebraska, had joined the faculty as an industrial arts teacher. *Front row, left to right*: Murray Francescato, Teresa (Tess) McGinn, Lorena Pachelli, Ms. McFarland, Katherine Reye. *Back row, left to right*: John J. Sebben Jr., Amy Skidmore, Eugene McGinn, Anthony Faoro. *Photo courtesy of Faoro Family Photo Archives.*

Opposite, top: Houses that matched the snow! After the second school was removed from the lot at the corner of Dexter Street and Wolcott Avenue, three two-bedroom houses were purchased from the town of Las Animas and moved to the site for faculty housing prior to 1953. Their exteriors were asbestos shingles, and they each had a coal-burning furnace. The initial inhabitants included Martin and Shirley Anzelini and their children in 1953–54; Anthony and Estella Faoro from 1953 to 1962; Ralph Fausone and Murray Francescato during the mid-1950s and into the 1960s. As the icicles suggest, there was little insulation, and a letter from Shirley Anzelini attests to this: "The heating bill was so high and still cold—so we went back to my mom's." *Photo courtesy of Faoro Family Photo Archives.*

With temporary/short-term residents and an arid landscape, growing a lawn was not a priority, so only the Faoros' faculty home had a front lawn and flower beds, along with a fence to keep both kids and collie from the main street that ran in front of the houses. *Photo courtesy of Faoro Family Photo Archives.*

Mary and Lawrence Terry both took on the job of janitor for the gym, and Mary was a cook as well. Their son, Sam (who lived next door to them), and his family contributed to the team effort while remaining active in school and sports. Sam's daughter Lois remembers being the one to clean the gym one night, finding her imagination running a bit wild and feeling terrified of every sound the furnace and building made, even though she knew that many eyes watched over her small town and very little went unnoticed. *Photo courtesy of Faoro Family Photo Archives.*

Opposite, top: Mining was in his blood! As unlandscaped or poorly landscaped as the front yards were, the backyards were even more so, making it possible to play in the dirt for hours. As the grandson of a miner, this little boy had a notation in his baby book indicating he could play independently for up to half an hour with his sand pail and shovel. These early beginnings got him all the way to a degree from Colorado School of Mines. *Photo courtesy of Faoro Family Photo Archives.*

Opposite, bottom: Mary and Angelo Zancanaro were two foundation blocks of the community in their own quiet ways. Mary was a cook in the school lunch program and was remembered for her innovative kindness as well as her lunches. In a time before free and reduced lunch, commercial dishwashers and prepared foods, Mary made sure that no child went hungry and devised a plan that a willingness to wash dishes for fifteen minutes of your recess would allow you to eat for free. Even students who had lunch money could choose this option and keep their cash to have as a bit of spending money for leisure times, remembers Chuck Cambruzzi. Angelo was the lead janitor for the school and a member of the community band. *Photo courtesy of Shirley Compton and Zancanaro Family Photo Archives.*

staff positions were frequently locals, including the Zancanaro family: Mary helped prepare the daily lunch, Angelo taught shop classes and both were involved as janitors. Lawrence and Mary Terry and their son Sam's family were also employed in janitorial positions, and Mary was involved with the food service.

The typical home in Main Sopris had a "shotgun" floor plan with a covered porch and two to three rooms laid out in a straight line with no connecting hallways. The living room was located at the front of the house, followed by the sleeping area, then the kitchen at the back of the house. The exterior was almost always stucco, and the interior walls were lath and plaster. Since the original homes predated indoor plumbing, each home had an outhouse, and in this rural area, the yards often included chicken coops,

A shotgun-style house on Sullivan Street (*upper left*). "Shotgun style" refers to a house plan that has the front and back doors aligned and three sequential rooms, beginning at the front door with a parlor or living room, followed by sleeping quarters and then a kitchen with "dinner table" space at the rear of the house. An outhouse provided the bathroom function, at a distance from the house. Even though each house faced a defined street, it was far more common for neighbors and friends to enter through the back/kitchen door. In time, sun porches were added and cellars were dug out pail by pail. *Photo courtesy of Faoro Family Photo Archives.*

Old-country traditions included an outdoor oven for baking several loaves of bread at one time. In Italian, it is a *forno* (reflected in the names of such dishes as ziti al forno) and it is called an *horno* (pronounced "OR-no") when describing the outdoor oven made of adobe bricks and covered with a coating of plaster found in the Southwest and used by the Native Americans and early settlers, often from Mexico. In addition to not heating up the house to bake bread on hot summer days, fornos filled the air with amazing aromas. Jennie Incitti lived just west of the school gym and diagonally across the intersection from the school, and students remember the smell of her baking bread invading their classrooms if the windows were open. *Photo courtesy of Monique Hartman and Incitti Family Photo Archives.*

rabbit hutches and shanties. Many also had an outdoor oven, the beehive-shaped *forno* of the Italian culture or the *horno* of the Mexican culture. Some had brick structures that included an outdoor oven and a metal grill for cooking meats. Wine cellars were also an important feature, and several were added after the house was built by digging out a basement under the existing structure. As families grew, the simple structures no longer met their needs, so additional rooms and, later, bathrooms, were added, in addition to freestanding garages that doubled as workshops when cars became the norm. Most men had carpentry skills, so they upgraded their wives' kitchens to include running water and custom cabinets with new laminate countertops.

The one exception to the shotgun floor plan was the house on the northeast corner of James Avenue and Sullivan Street, known initially as

Above: When indoor plumbing and electricity became available to the homes of Sopris in the 1930s, it was the perfect time for a kitchen remodel. The men of Sopris had grown up learning carpentry skills from their fathers and grandfathers, and they gained additional skills as part of their training in their industrial arts classes in school, so when the need to remodel and modernize arose, they replaced sideboards and pantry cupboards with built-in cabinets that had laminate tops, held in place by metal edging. Jennie Faoro's kitchen had a window that looked into a sunporch where her treadle sewing machine was kept and where African violets bloomed. A bathroom was added to most, but not all, homes. *Photo courtesy of Faoro Family Photo Archives.*

Opposite: Martin and Elsie Komora, born in Austria and Germany, arrived in the United States in 1883, initially settling in Illinois before making their way west to Colorado in 1900 with their children, Frank, William, Clara and Albert. Their family continued to grow with the addition of Thomas in 1900 and Mary in 1904. They originally settled in Piedmont, where Martin was employed by Rocky Mountain Fuel Company as a blacksmith. He became an employee of CF&I in June 1909, and shortly thereafter, the family relocated from Piedmont to Main Sopris, eventually residing in the beautiful sandstone home on the northeast corner of Sullivan Street and James Avenue. *Photo courtesy of Lory Nelson Greaves and Komora Family Photo Archives.*

the Komora residence and later as the home of Emma Watson. Unlike the other homes of the neighborhood, it was of sandstone, two rooms wide, and featured a hip roof that extended over a covered porch supported by large columns. Like the other homes, it had shanties and sheds for outdoor storage and an outhouse.

Chapter 5

JERRYVILLE

THE ORIGINS

Jerryville? Farrelville? Jerry Farrell Ville? While those still living knew the neighborhood as Jerryville, the legal property descriptions on the warranty deeds created when the homes were purchased by the United States government in 1968 still read "Farrelville." Many spellings appear throughout the documented history of the neighborhood—Farrlville, Farreleville, Farrellville—all referring to the same fifteen blocks. But why "Farelleville"? Was it his outrageous Irish antics or perhaps the end-of-the-workweek trips to a local watering hole that so endeared Jerry Farrell to his employees and friends that they would name the town after him? Was it luck that brought him to the area, advice from friends or advice from the family of Gertrude Staples, who became his wife on November 18, 1888? (See the Farlville plat map in Appendix A.)

In 1895, Jerry Farrell finalized a land patent for forty acres just a bit north of the patents filed by Sopris and Littlefield, and while little is known of the neighborhood's early history, the plat for "Farrlville" was certified by Fred N. Archibald, surveyor, on July 10, 1888, and recorded by Eugenio Garcia, deputy recorder of Las Animas County, on August 17, 1888.[72] Unlike the plat filings for St. Thomas and Sopris, no one is designated as having hired Archibald to do the plat, so those interests remain unknown. On a later warranty deed, Farrellville is referred to as a St. Thomas addition; on another, it is referenced as an addition to Sopris.

In 1889, Farrellville appears on the Sopris Mine No. 4 map, along with Sopris and St. Thomas, implying it was part of the sale of the mines held by the Denver Fuel Company as CF&I was formed, yet on August 29, 1913, a "quit-claim" deed was filed indicating that Rocky Mountain Fuel Company of both Colorado and Wyoming received one hundred dollars in exchange for releasing to Frederick A.A. Williams many lots in Farrellville with the following restrictions:

> *The parties of the first part* [the Rocky Mountain Fuel Co.]… *whereof is hereby confessed and acknowledged, have remised, released, sold, conveyed and* QUIT-CLAIMED…*forever, all the right, title, interest, claim and demand which the said parties of the first part have in and to the surface only of the following described lots or parcels of land…in the Town of Farrellville according to the plat thereof of record.…*
>
> *Saving, excepting and reserving…all of the coal and other minerals in, underlying or beneath the surface of all singular lots or parcels of land above described and conveyed…*

This document implies that the plat was done by the Rocky Mountain Fuel Company and it owned all the land, even though Rocky Mountain Fuel Company does not appear on the plat document. A total of over one hundred lots on Main, First and Second Streets, and entire blocks between Second and Fourth Streets were included in the transaction—essentially, most of the town (see the Farrellville plat map in Appendix A). Perhaps Farrellville appears on the "Colorado Fuel and Iron Company's Sopris Mine #4" map because the Sopris Mine No. 4 tunnels were so close to the section of land where Farrellville was located.

Who was Frederick A.A. Williams? He was at times referred to as F.A.A. Williams, and advertisements by F.A.A. Williams appear in the *Polk's Trinidad City Directory* over several years, stating, "Investments for non-residents in loans or real estate a specialty," and giving his address as Room 2, Odd Fellows Block, Trinidad.

Just after the release of the mineral rights to the lots, on September 23, 1913, a campaign to unionize the miners was taken up again. Much like during the 1901 to 1904 attempt, the militia was called in to assist. This strike, however, turned out very differently.

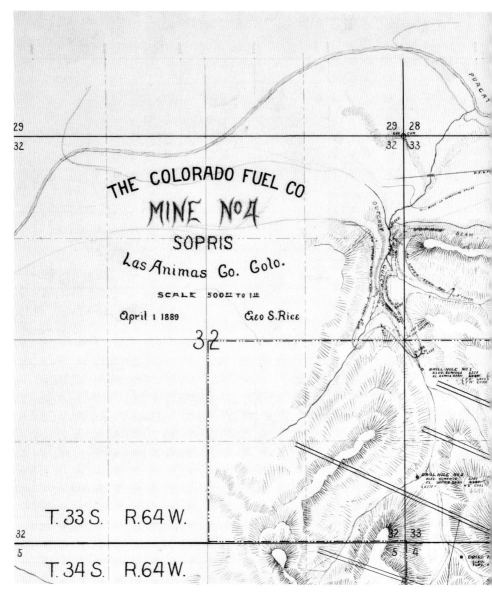

Even though the St. Thomas and Sopris neighborhoods were established by the Denver Fuel Company, they were quickly sold and became part of the merger that created the Colorado Fuel and Iron Company. This cropped image emphasizes the relationships in size and location between Sopris, St. Thomas and Jerryville/Farrelville and shows how extensive the mine tunnel network was in that area. *Map courtesy of Steelworks Center of the West, Bessemer Historical Society, Pueblo, Colorado.*

JERRYVILLE AND THE COAL FIELD WARS

During the strike of 1913–14, the camps became the sites of guerrilla warfare and were divided into districts. Jerryville was considered to be part of the Starkville-Piedmont-Sopris district and "the union hornet's nest of this district."[73] Each miner had to purchase his own dynamite and blasting powder for work, and the miners were able to use that inventory during the strike for new purposes. In an article carried in many state newspapers, Captain Hildreth Frost stated, "The activists seem to be using the Rock Saloon in Jerryville as a safe place to plan and execute violent and intimidating acts to discourage non-union miners from going into the mines, and to disrupt the supply chain that allowed the coal to get to the steel mill and other customers."[74] Among the "dastardly deeds" the union organizers were said to

Jerryville/Farrellville was considered to be the "union's hornet nest in the district," and the Rock House Saloon was the "beehive of union activity" (*Chronicle News*, August 27, 1914) during the strike of 1913–14. It was an easily identified landmark in Jerryville, located just next to the home of Crist Cunico Sr., and was said to be where union advocates met to plan their next guerrilla warfare attack, according to an article in the local press. One might wonder how such rumors were spread and published, and it seems that there was espionage within the ranks. Years later, the Rock House Saloon (*pictured*) remained, and young cousins Crist Cunico and Bernie Morgan likely had adventures exploring it. *Photo courtesy of Christina Cunico Miller and Cunico Family Photo Archives.*

be plotting was an explosion within a mine while the "scab" miners were at work, accessing a mine tunnel in the Piedmont mine from a little-known well in Jerryville; the plan was discovered and was not carried out.[75]

To add to the drama, the camps had their own double agent, who was drawing an income from both the miners' compensation fund and the mine operators. Antone Langowski, a resident of the Ludlow Tent Colony, had shared with the sheriff of Sopris, Monty (Montgomery) Masingale, that he wished to leave the union and return to work, even though he was the secretary-treasurer of the local union. Masingale suggested he remain active and try to prevent the vandalism and property damage that had marked the conflict so far, offering to pay him three dollars per day for reporting plans in advance, to which Antone agreed. At the same time, he was receiving three dollars per week from the union in strike benefits. When the miners realized what was going on, they were understandably angry at one of their own turning against them. Surely violence would have ensued had Langowski not had a militiaman escort him to Denver to testify in front of the congressional investigating committee, fearing for his life if the miners got to him first.[76]

MOVING FORWARD

As with all the neighborhoods of Sopris, there was some movement of families from one neighborhood to the other due to marriage, changing family sizes, business opportunities or loss of homes to fire. Jerryville was no exception. John Baptiste Cunico arrived in the United States in 1899 from Asiago, Italy, and married Maria Borgo in 1902. After working in the mines for many years, John Baptiste purchased the original Brunelli grocery store in Jerryville after the mine explosion of 1922.[77] His sudden death from an infection (rabies) that developed after he was bitten by the family cat in 1937 led to the store being taken over by his son, Louis "Binda" Cunico.[78] Binda and Angie (Incitti), along with their sons John and Robert, operated the store until 1970, when the Army Corps of Engineers required them to move. Binda's mother, Maria, lived with Binda's family until her death in 1966.

During the properties buyout in 1968, an offer was made to relocate the Cunico Store, but its customer base had been fragmented to the point that many loyal customers were no longer within the local market, and there would have been established stores in any new location it might try to gain

John Batiste Cunico came to the United States from Asiago, in northern Italy, with a cousin as the mines were recruiting workers. He married Marie Bargo in 1902, and they became the parents of seven children. After being fortunate enough to survive two mine explosions, Giovanni/John decided it was time to take up a new line of work, so he bought the original Brunelli Store in Farrellville/Jerryville from Frank Brunelli when Brunelli relocated his business to the St. Thomas neighborhood. *Front row, left to right*: Julia, Catherine, Crist, Esther. *Back row, left to right*: Marie, Angelo, John Batiste, Louis (Binda). *Photo courtesy of Christina Cunico Miller and Cunico Family Photo Archives.*

Neighborhood stores existed in each neighborhood except Piedmont after the mines closed. As the signage indicates, this store was owned and operated by the Cunico family—initially by Giovanni Batista Cunico and his wife, Marie, and then their son Louis and his wife, Angie Incitti. Giovanni Batista met an untimely death in July 1937 as the result of being bitten by a house cat that carried rabies. The family then decided that Louis "Binda" Cunico and his family would be in charge of the store and that their mother would reside with them. Binda and Angie welcomed walk-in customers, but Binda also strongly believed in customer service, so he spent the morning stopping by the homes of his customers to personally take their orders before heading to the wholesale houses in Trinidad to secure anything not currently in inventory. Once the orders were packaged, he spent his afternoon delivering them to the families. When they were old enough to see over the steering wheel, his sons Johnny and Bobby made the deliveries. *Photo courtesy of Christina Cunico Miller and Cunico Family Photo Archives.*

customers from. Timing also played a roll, because the Cunicos' sons, Bob and John, graduated that year from Trinidad High School and Trinidad State Junior College respectively, and both boys were heading to Colorado State University in Fort Collins. Angie and Binda chose to relocate to Fort Collins, Colorado, as well, rather than choosing to relocate the store.[79]

Cristiano (Crist) and Pena (Mary Ella Ferri) Cunico, Binda's older brother and his wife, also remained in Jerryville until the end, along with Pena's sister, Gina, and Gina's husband, Carl Amato. Their homes had been company homes that were purchased and renovated.

While many of the miners were from Europe, James Daily was born in Mississippi—the son of freed slaves—and came to Sopris from Butler County, Kansas, with his wife and two sons between 1900 and 1910. The

As the mining companies closed their local mines and reallocated their resources, the company houses were purchased by those wanting to remain in the area. Such was the case with the home of Crist and Pena Cunico in Jerryville. *Photo courtesy of Christina Cunico Miller and Cunico Family Photo Archives.*

This small adobe home was modified to include a covered porch, a large window and even a glass-brick corner enclosure (not shown) that added natural light. Large trees grew to shade the yard and home, and white stucco covered the adobe exterior. *Photo courtesy of Christina Cunico Miller and Cunico Family Photo Archives.*

1900 census shows them running a boardinghouse in Walnut, Kansas, and the 1910 census records James's occupation as engineer at the waterworks plant. The Daily family had grown to three children with the arrival of their daughter that year. By the mid-1950s, the Daily home was located next door to Crist and Pena Cunico. James lost his wife when the children were in their teens and became a widower and single parent. The Cunico grandchildren remember him fondly as a kind neighbor and friend, always willing to share from his fruit trees.

Jerryville was always a small and close community, and by the time of the buyout in 1968, fifty properties had to be purchased by the government, representing the holdings of thirty-one families. A list of former residents can be found in Appendix B.

Chapter 6

PIEDMONT

THE MINES

Farthest east from Main Sopris, Piedmont was repeatedly linked to other nearby communities when the census was taken. It was included in the census linked to Jansen in Precinct 19 when Theresa Sardello was the enumerator in 1930; to Precinct 18, which included North Starkville, in 1940 when Dominic Karcich was the enumerator; and to Holloway in 1950 when Frank Martinez was the enumerator.[80]

Unlike St. Thomas and Sopris, the Piedmont mine was a Rocky Mountain Fuel Company mine that appears in the 1903 biennial state mining inspector's report as a "new mine" in May, and it reported almost twelve thousand tons of coal mined between June and October before shutting down due to a strike in November and December.[81] President Edward Edgar Shumway was a Nebraska farmer who came to Colorado to work in the hay and grain market. Customers who needed hay and grain also needed wood and coal, so he added those products to his line. The demand was so encouraging that he took on a partner and bought out the Stewart Coal & Lime Company in 1891. In 1894, the company name was changed to Rocky Mountain Fuel Company, operating out of Denver, and immediately purchased eight mines along the Front Range and on the Western Slope.[82]

Shumway died from injuries received while investigating the damage caused by and the source of the explosion of his Vulcan mine, and leadership

Top: The life of a miner's wife was anything but glamorous—living in an isolated coal camp, between rolling hills covered with juniper, cedar, cacti and plants that required little water, in a small adobe house on a patch of dirt, with little or no privacy to escape to outside the walls of her home. Her days were filled with the family's needs for food and care in a non-mechanized world. The no. 3 tubs hanging on the nearest house met multiple needs—as a bathtub on Saturday nights, as a laundry tub in combination with a washboard or as a rain barrel to collect rainwater if it fell. If she could read and write, it was likely her responsibility to teach her children and maybe the children of others living in the camp. *Photo courtesy of Carnegie Library for Local History— Boulder Public Library, Boulder, Colorado.*

Bottom: "Looking the land o'er" from the water tower or the tipple, we see just how interconnected the miners and the mines were with the houses and shops just a short distance away. The need for timber to support the roofs of the mines, extend the track for the pit cars within the mines and repair the track for the coal cars far exceeded the wood available from the small juniper and spruce that dominated the landscape, so it was necessary to seek another source, and that source was often nearby Catskill, New Mexico. *Photo courtesy of Carnegie Library for Local History—Boulder Public Library, Boulder, Colorado.*

Sixteen tons is only the beginning of what this mine produced during its lifetime, from opening in July 1903 to no longer being included in state mining reports after 1922. Despite the strike of 1903–4 that closed it down after just three months as a new mine, and other strikes through the years, this Rocky Mountain Fuel Company mine produced a total of 1,984,427 tons of coal. Lying in the Raton Basin—which is composed of the Raton and Vermejo formations that are found in Las Animas County, Colorado, and Colfax County, New Mexico—Piedmont mine contained seven veins; the Piedmont vein was consistently between four and a half and six feet wide. After the early strike, and working to capacity, in 1905, over 10,428,301 tons of coal were produced by Colorado's mines, with Piedmont contributing 30,472 tons. *Photo courtesy of Carnegie Library for Local History—Boulder Public Library, Boulder, Colorado.*

passed to David W. Brown in 1914 and then to John J. Roche, one of the original officers of the company, in 1922. After John Roche's death in 1927, management was taken over by his daughter, Josephine Roche.[83] In contrast to her father's staunchly anti-union beliefs, Josephine was educated at Vassar and spent time with Jane Addams at Hull House before completing a master's degree in social work at Columbia University. Because of her beliefs regarding the positive aspects of unionism, as well as her concern for the working class, she often found herself at odds with other mine owners, including Rockefeller.[84]

A November 2, 1912 newspaper article states:

> *It is reported that the Rocky Mountain Fuel Company is negotiating for the purchase of the controlling interest in the St. Louis, Rocky Mountain & Pacific company, which owns extensive coal fields in Southern Colorado and Northern New Mexico. In 1905 the majority stockholders of the St. Louis, Rocky Mountain & Pacific placed their holdings in a voting*

trust until 1915. Last week the voting trust was dissolved and the stock distributed to five trustees, who are given the right to sell the entire amount for $7,500,000. The trustees hold 75 percent of the $10,000,000 stock of the corporation.[85]

This seems to match the timeline of the aggressive purchase of Jerryville lots and mineral rights. According to the 1915 mining report, Rocky Mountain Fuel Company had only the Piedmont mine, and by 1917, Labelle Mine had been added to the company's holdings, with William Morgan as the superintendent of both. In 1918, the list of mines in Las Animas County owned by Rocky Mountain Fuel Company included Forbes 4 and Forbes 9, Southwestern in Aguilar and Labelle and Piedmont in Sopris, but by 1920, the company had only one Forbes mine, and by 1923, Piedmont mine was no longer listed as an operating mine. The 1924 report listed only Forbes and Southwestern as mines operated by Rocky Mountain Fuel Company in Southern Colorado, in addition to the company's many mines in Weld and Boulder Counties farther north. Between 1931 and 1934, the Labelle mine was leased or sold to William Morgan, and with the mines closed, the miners found it necessary to commute to nearby mines owned by Colorado Fuel and Iron counterparts.

THE TOWN

When the mines closed, the homes were sold to those wishing to remain in the community, including the Mincic family. Until the end, the Piedmont Tavern, owned by Tony and Catherine Maccagnan (also known as Mac's Place and Cate's Place by some), was a gathering place for all. Tony Maccagnan arrived from Fonzaso in northern Italy in 1913 and worked beside others from that small village as he learned English and formed friendships. He married Catherine Cunico of Jerryville on October 24, 1922. Catherine was born in the United States but traveled to Asiago, Italy, with her mother and siblings at age three or four and lived there for four years before returning to the United States. Thirteen years after marrying, Tony and Catherine purchased property from Constante and Lucy Ossola and established the Piedmont Tavern.[86]

The Piedmont Tavern was the place to be on a Saturday night if you wanted to dance or spend time with friends. Angie (Incitti) Cunico, sister-in-law to Catherine, was an accomplished accordion player. Along with other young

Above: A new generation will grow up in Piedmont, at least until the dam makes her move. Lee Mincic was the first of the Mincics' sons to be born in the United States. He graduated from Lincoln High School in Sopris and served in the Air Force during the Korean War. When he returned home, he worked for the Colorado and Southern Railroad, which hauled the coal from the mines. He continued to be promoted in his career, becoming the bridge crew foreman before his retirement. He and his wife, Mary Louise (Ferraro), were the parents of two children, whom they raised in the neighborhood Lee had grown up in, near his parents. *Photo courtesy of Charlie Mincic and Mincic Family Photo Archives.*

Opposite, top: Achieving the American Dream! Tony Macagnan (*with bottle and flowers*) is joined by his sister-in-law Annie and her husband, Felix; his mother-in-law, Marie Cunico; and his wife, Catherine, as he celebrates the opening of the Piedmont Tavern and dance hall. The Piedmont tavern was the place to be on a Saturday night if you wanted to dance or spend time with friends. Tony and Catherine had two sons and a daughter, and with Catherine's mother and siblings near, the children never lacked opportunities to play with cousins. *Photo courtesy of Maccagnan & DeAngelis Family Photo Archives.*

Who can resist the music of an accordion? Angie Incitti learned to play the accordion from her father, and after marrying Binda (Louis) Cunico, she became Catherine Cunico Maccagnan's sister-in-law. Angie and other young musicians in the community often gathered at the Piedmont Tavern to play together and eventually formed an ensemble named the Star Dusters. *Photo courtesy of Monique Hartman and Incitti Family Photo Archives.*

talent from the various neighborhoods, Angie's band, the Star Dusters, provided great music in the 1950s. It is estimated that a Saturday crowd at Piedmont Tavern would be in the neighborhood of 150 people.

Piedmont Tavern was also the place of choice for local wedding receptions, allowing the children access to the pinball machine and other games and the men an escape from dancing to play bocce in the bocce alleys beyond the bar.

As a very small neighborhood, Piedmont enjoyed significant diversity and a blending of heritages. Families represented five foreign countries (Italy, Austria, Wales, Romania and Mexico) and four states other than Colorado (Texas, Oklahoma, New Mexico and New Jersey). The immigrant parents did not know English, and the women often chose not to learn English, so the children were reliant on friends and school to gain English skills while still needing to communicate with their parents and grandparents in their native language.

PART III

THE PURGATOIRE RIVER

Chapter 1

TOO MUCH OF A GOOD THING

Rain is essential to Southern Colorado's economy, yet rainfall is historically unpredictable, with wide swings from year to year. Las Animas County is at an elevation between 4,321 feet and 13,962 feet; the weather station at Trinidad Lake is at 6,310 feet. Average rainfall between 1898 and 1970 was 15.05 inches (compared to a national average of almost 40 inches); the lowest recorded precipitation was 2.73 inches, in 1908, and the highest recorded precipitation was 24.25 inches, in 1915. Almost half the years between 1900 and 1968 had below-average rainfall. The area is arid, with bragging rights to 265 sunny days per year and a xeriscape landscape of cacti, piñon pine, cedar, sagebrush and flowering plants such as Indian paintbrush, sunflowers, peace pipes and honeysuckle.

The Purgatoire River—sometimes referred to as the Purgatory River, Las Animas River or Picketwire River—originates in the Culebra Range of the nearby Sangre de Cristo Mountains; its three forks merge near Weston to become a single 196-mile-long river that flows through the mining camps of Segundo, Primero, Valdez and—until 1970—Sopris. From there, it continues toward the center of Trinidad, moving past Jansen on Highway 12. As its journey continues, it eventually flows into the Arkansas River about 50 miles from the Kansas state line, and the Arkansas River carries its waters east into Kansas. The total area of the Purgatoire River Basin is 2,206,204 acres or 3,447 square miles.

The livelihoods of those in Sopris who lived along the river and owned water rights depended on the waters of the Purgatoire. At Sopris Plaza, and farther east of Trinidad into the Sunflower Valley, the river provided water to irrigate the land and bring it to life as crops and as pasture for their animals. While rain is essential to the area, occasionally—and without warning—the Purgatoire took on far more water than it could keep within its banks, flooding fields and damaging property. A fine line existed between what was needed and "too much," and because the three forks of the Purgatoire originate in the mountains, it was not only local rainfall that impacted the river but also snowmelt and mountain rains miles away. As the forks join, the volume of water increases, and as the tributaries of Riley Canyon and Long Canyon enter the Purgatoire, just to the west of Sopris, the volume increases exponentially. When this was combined with unpredictable cloudbursts or days of rain in this arid land, the result was a powerful surge of water that moved through Sopris and into Trinidad, wreaking havoc along its path.

As cross-country train travelers have noticed, where the rivers go, the trains go, and the banks of the Purgatoire and the Arkansas were no exception, with train tracks not far from the banks of both. As a result, floods inevitably washed out the train tracks, stranding passengers and halting the movement of freight and commodities.

The typical depth of the Purgatoire as it passed through Sopris was less than three feet, but if rain lasted for hours or days, that could change quickly. As the United States' rail system expanded, before the interstate highway system and air travel, trains were how people and things got from place to place. Each time a flood happened, the train companies experienced major losses, and history repeated itself again and again. Significant floods of record occurred in 1875, 1881, 1886, 1903, 1904, 1908, 1909, 1914, 1925, 1942, 1954, 1955 and 1965; others are referenced but not documented in the newspapers of the day. Many of the floods led to loss of life, and all led to destruction of property and disruption of commerce and mail delivery as the high waters raced down the usually shallow riverbed, taking parts of the bank and vegetation with them. This debris, moving at great speed, created battering rams that crashed into and released bridges and train tracks from their moorings and footings; tore down utility poles; wiped out telegraph, phone and electrical lines; damaged crops; and uprooted fenceposts. Each flood devastated the area's infrastructure, forcing bridges to be completely rebuilt, railroad tracks to be reestablished on solid ground, roads—used for wagons and coaches in the nineteenth century and automobiles in the later years—to be made navigable again and buildings damaged by the floods rebuilt.

Documentation of these floods in the nineteenth century consists of personal diaries and stories published in newspapers, but in 1904, there were floods throughout the United States, and the severity of the many floods led to a nationwide report by the U.S. Geological Survey that included photos of the damage in Trinidad in addition to other states. Photography and camera clubs had become popular by the 1920s, and we are fortunate to have images of floods in the twentieth century. A chronological record of Purgatoire floods follows, documented by area newspapers and Associated Press stories picked up by newspapers in adjacent states. Occasionally, there is a reference to a previous flood as a basis of comparison.

Chapter 2

MAJOR FLOODS OF THE
PURGATOIRE RIVER

SATURDAY, SEPTEMBER 25, 1875

The flood was reported to have wiped out over 70 miles of roadbed, all the way to Ft. Dodge, Kansas; the river rose five to six feet in just two hours.[87]

SATURDAY, FEBRUARY 12, 1881

Unusually warm weather and winter rain throughout west Las Animas County led to rising water levels that caused the Purgatoire to rise above its banks and flood nearby tracks of the Santa Fe Railroad.

Rather than cresting and receding, the river continued to increase in volume until the next evening, stranding trains headed East.

It is reported that three to four miles of track continued to be under four feet of water and the Purgatoire bridge could not be crossed....

"It was anticipated that it would be Monday before the trains would be able to reach Denver."[88]

THURSDAY, APRIL 22, 1886

[This flood was] *the result of several days of rain which caused the Purgatoire to go over its banks in Trinidad at 3:00 a.m., forcing people to evacuate in the middle of the night desperate to reach higher ground in darkness. One life was lost. It also flooded the water-works plant, polluting the city's water supply. Property damage is estimated at $18,000.*[89]

FRIDAY, AUGUST 20, 1886

Days of rain coming down in torrents that began on August 17, 1886 stranded six trains between Colorado and Kansas City. While the story of each train is not known, a passenger shared his experiences with the Kansas City Times *after safely returning to his point of origin.*

Two trains left Kansas City a short time apart on Tuesday morning and both found themselves and their nearly 200 passengers stranded by midday Wednesday near Caddoa (just across the Kansas state line) as the Arkansas River took on water from the Purgatoire.

The engineers had hoped to reverse course and return to safety, but before authorization to reverse course was received, water had risen behind them. With high water over the tracks both in front and behind, they were stranded.

The dining car had no food to speak of, but the train was hauling an express car that contained perishables and the crew took out processed beef that they were able to prepare over an open fire in the section house. That evening they had the same menu and were grateful for it.

By morning that small building had become partially submerged, but the innovative and resourceful crew prepared the remaining meals by building small fires in the engine's firebox. When the waters receded enough to move about, the conductor ventured into a nearby town and located a source of bread, which thereafter was brought to the train each day by wagon.

When the construction train finally reached them, the crew chose to lay new track rather than attempting to salvage the damaged sections. Both trains returned to Kansas City on Saturday.

An evening train traveling the same route on Tuesday found itself stranded much farther East and on much lower ground. As the water rose rapidly, violently washing the track behind them away, the conductor realized that he must break free so that the train was not pulled into the waters. Using a crowbar, he removed track to isolate the train where it stood leaving over one-quarter mile of track behind the train in case it needed to move back a bit.

Unlike the morning trains, the evening train was not pulling an express car and all passengers had almost nothing to eat for the 36 hours that they were stranded. By Thursday they were able to return to Kansas City.

Full repair of the tracks and roadways was anticipated to take a month in time and cost the Santa Fe Railroad no less than one-half million dollars.[90]

TUESDAY, JUNE 9, 1903

The Purgatoire River rose three feet (as a result of steady rain), and then experienced a ten-foot wall of water as the river crested, flooding the boulevard and doing significant damage below the city and flooding the lowlands.[91]

FRIDAY, SEPTEMBER 30, 1904

Moderate rain began to fall at the source of the Purgatoire River on Tuesday, September 27 and continued for two days, growing more intense as it continued, ultimately wreaking havoc on more than 30 blocks of residential and business properties in Trinidad after damaging properties all along the river's path through the mining camps of the upper drainage area.

The railroad companies all experienced significant loss. The Colorado and Southern railroad bed on Riley Canyon was badly damaged and the C&S lost a total of 24 bridges and an estimated 10,000 railroad ties in Colorado and the extended routes.

"In Sopris, one bridge owned by the Colorado and Wyoming Railroad is so weakened that it may fall, and two miles of track are washed out between Sopris and Jansen. The Santa Fe Railroad has one-thousand feet of track in the river at Jansen, and the bridge at Starkville is washed away."

In Trinidad, with a population of 5,000, the water reached two to four feet in depth in the city, impacting at least 30 blocks of residences and businesses. The rushing waters ate away at the riverbank, causing damage to many businesses adjacent to the Purgatoire, including a boarding house, the new Baca Hotel, and the Harvey House Restaurant and hotel.

Farther from the river, it is said that the Colorado Supply company on lower Commercial Street has lost $10,000 worth of inventory stored in the basement.

Western Union and the U.S. Postal telegraph system were both badly damaged, making communication difficult at first, and then impossible.

According to a witness at the Cardenas Hotel, the river continued to rise Thursday afternoon and evening, but it remained below the bank until the rains reached cloudburst intensity at about 8:30 p.m. By 2:30 a.m. on Friday it had risen above the bank and was two feet deep on the lawn of the Cardenas and within a few inches of the door. Those living along the river were alerted to the flood danger as warning shots from revolvers rang out followed by the fire alarm and train and shop whistles throughout town. The waters continued to rise for two more hours, before there were indications it was receding.

It was estimated that the damages from the flood would equal a million dollars, at least.[92]

No trains today, or for many more days, thanks to the flood of 1904. As the Purgatoire River flood passed through, it not only washed away the bank on the south side but also carried away all but one wall of the train station, which had recently been built at a cost of $15,000. It is seen here with its roof almost collapsed; the Harvey House Restaurant next door was badly damaged. Damage from the flood was estimated to be $1 million at least. The Colorado Supply Company, located on lower Commercial Street, estimated a loss of inventory worth $10,000. The Baca brothers were about to complete a $20,000 hotel near the Commercial Street bridge; by morning, the entire building site was washed clean (*Topeka State Journal*, October 1, 1904). *Photo courtesy of History Colorado, Stephen H. Hart Research Center.*

Right next door to the Santa Fe Depot, the Cardenas Hotel escaped significant damage. Witnesses confirmed that the river continued to rise on Thursday afternoon and evening, but it remained below its banks until the rains reached cloudburst intensity at about eight thirty. By two thirty on Friday morning, it had risen above its banks and was two feet deep on the Cardenas's lawn and within a few inches of the door. *Photo courtesy of History Colorado, Stephen H. Hart Research Center.*

After the 1904 flood, additional steps were taken to reinforce the banks of the Purgatoire in front of the Cardenas Hotel. In August 1905, the Santa Fe Company, which owned the Cardenas, committed to expanding and improving the property, and in 1914, Mary Jane Colter, an architect and designer from Kansas City employed by the Fred Harvey Company, came to Trinidad to oversee additional modifications and renovations. *Photo courtesy of History Colorado, Stephen H. Hart Research Center.*

THURSDAY, JULY 16, 1908

Rain began steadily on Tuesday afternoon and by 6:00 p.m. on Wednesday night the Purgatoire was rising rapidly and continued for two days, reminding many of the flood just four years prior that completely washed away the Santa Fe Depot.

The heaviest rains were reported in Riley Canyon, where the stream exceeded its banks and washed away several small adobe houses and flooded other buildings.

Those flood waters entered the Purgatoire causing damage at Segundo, Sopris and Jansen before entering Trinidad and once again eating away the riverbank near the Santa Fe Depot.

Knowing the destruction of 1904 and that several smaller bridges outside of Trinidad had already been washed away, a special patrol from the local police department was assigned to rope off the bridges to keep people from crossing them.[93]

THURSDAY, AUGUST 18, 1909

A sudden cloudburst near Trinidad resulted in a floodwater that washed away several bridges and several miles of Colorado and Southern Railway tracks. A force of men was put to work filling sandbags to attempt to keep the river in its banks in the many places where the concrete wall had given way. Observers said that the damage was the worst since the flood of 1904.[94]

THURSDAY, JULY 23, 1914

Several days of rain have again flooded the Purgatoire and endangered the properties of those living along its banks. Recently those landowners petitioned the city council asking that reinforced dikes or cribs be built to prevent the repeated problem of flooding. So desperate were the landowners that they agreed to put up a portion of the needed funds to subsidize the budget of the street and bridge fund.[95]

WEDNESDAY, JULY 22, 1925

A sudden cloudburst on July 22 drove the Purgatoire into a state of rage washing away bridges and train tracks, flooding basements, and eroding the highways to the tune of $400,000 in damage.

By morning, the sky was clear and sunny as people who had to take refuge on higher ground in boarding houses and hotels returned to assess the damage to their properties.

As is often the case, the railroads sustained the most significant damage. The Atchison Topeka & Santa Fe Railroad lost 600 feet of track and a steel bridge necessary to run the route between Chicago and California; additional washouts have made it impossible for the Colorado and Southern and the Denver & Rio Grande to maintain their service, as well.

As the smaller, outlying communities assess their losses the total may well exceed the $400,000 in damages.[96]

THURSDAY, APRIL 23, 1942

Unusually warm weather led to early snowmelt in the mountains which caused an immediate increase in streamflow for all streams in Las Animas County.

Rain began to fall west of Trinidad in the mining areas along the river on April 23, and the Purgatoire, already carrying more water than usual, quickly swelled beyond the capacity of the banks to contain it.

By all accounts, this surge exceeded the 1904 flood which had a surge of 45,400 cubic feet per second.

Flood waters invaded 50 business and residential blocks in the center of the city, surrounding the jail and forcing evacuation through a jail window just before dawn. City Hall was also surrounded.

Several city-center bridges were damaged and the Chestnut Street bridge was washed away and piled up against the Colorado and Southern trestle which remained in place, even though the tracks approaching from the south had been washed out leaving the tracks in midair.

The Colorado & Southern train, traveling from Dallas to Denver, was held up at the station prior to the trestle washing out, keeping all passengers safe.

The Santa Fe's main tracks were under two feet of water and the Santa Fe train yards were under water for three-eighths of a mile.

By Saturday, the waters had receded, but the river continued to run full.

As communication resumed, it came to light that two lives were lost: Cicero Reeves, a 65-year-old rancher who drowned when he fell from his horse while trying to cross the river near his ranch 16 miles upriver from Trinidad and 5-year-old Jack Stoner who drowned when he fell into the flooded irrigation ditch on the family farm 13 miles east of Trinidad.[97]

FRIDAY, JULY 23, 1954

A rainfall of 1.42 inches fell rapidly in the Trinidad area, but excessive runoff was contained in the recently completed Piñon Canyon Dam located NW of the city.

Through the city, the Purgatoire was two feet from the top of the banks and retaining walls, but no damage was reported.[98]

TUESDAY, MAY 17, 1955

A steady rain began on Tuesday, May 17 throughout the Purgatoire River Valley west of Trinidad and continued for the next day and one-half, with a total accumulation of 3.5" falling in 36 hours.

The Purgatoire River that usually runs one to two feet deep was raging at 20–25 feet as it moved through Trinidad and on to the east through La Junta as it made its way to the Arkansas River and the John Martin Reservoir.

At least four states in the Southwest were heavily impacted by the rainfall, states that had been in the throes of a dustbowl just a month ago.

In Trinidad, a city with a population of just over 12,500, three homes along the Purgatoire were washed away, eventually closing State Highway 85-87 south of Trinidad when a 275' bridge was badly damaged by the current and after being battered by one of the three houses.

Four cross-town bridges were also washed away, leading to the death of a teenager, Anthony Roy Espinoza, who tried to drive across a bridge where the south end had been destroyed. His car was found the following day one mile downriver by the Linden Street bridge.

The Red Cross, working with the National Guard and city police, responded to the urgency and worked through the night to assisted in moving 500 families in the path of the flood to Trinidad State Junior College and a Catholic community center designated as safe accommodations.

The chairman of the Red Cross Disaster Committee, Charles Boustead, arranged for seven tank trucks from the Pueblo Ordinance Depot to haul 3,590 gallons of water to Trinidad, and for the Colorado state hospital in Pueblo to provide necessary blankets and medication.

Army officials at Ft. Carson provided food.

Four miles south, the surging waters of Raton Creek washed away the Sacred Heart church and three homes as it moved through Starkville. Damage was so severe that a local resident, writing to friends in Hutchinson, Kansas, suggested that damage in Starkville was so great, with homes filled with mud and partially destroyed, that he anticipated residents would not return to their homes and abandon the small town altogether.

Sopris Plaza, on the north side of the river, experienced significant flooding of the fields owned by the Blasi and Cuccia families, as shown in this photo. If you look closely, you can see the house and barn surrounded by water at the upper edge of the flood zone, by the large tree. The nearby bridge connecting Sopris Plaza to Sopris was completely washed away, and the train tracks sustained damage. *Photo courtesy of Faoro Family Photo Archives.*

To the east, the farming community of Hoehne is completely isolated due to washout of bridges and culverts, and to the west farmland and livestock were lost when the waters flooded crops and pastures, tearing down fences. Colorado's chief highway engineer, Mark U. Watrous, presented a conservative estimate of $520,000 dollars required for road repairs and Harold L. Smethills, regional director of the Small Business Administration, considered Trinidad and the Purgatoire valley to be a disaster area, making it eligible for emergency government loans.

The railroads again suffered major damage to tracks, bridges, and equipment. Ten railroad cars were toppled over when the depth of water in the Santa Fe railroad yard was enough to lift them and flip them. Tracks owned by each of the railroad companies were underwater and the ground beneath was washed away in many places. Many adjacent utility poles and telephone poles were toppled, leaving much of the city and surrounding towns without power and a means of communicating.

Waters began to recede rapidly by Saturday.[99]

Swing low… The train tracks approaching Starkville were undercut by the rushing waters, leaving several feet of track hanging just above the water in this spot and likely many other places. Such washouts prevented the coal trains from making their way to Trinidad and to the steel mill in Pueblo. *Photo courtesy of Faoro Family Photo Archives.*

"Looking across Pine Street—notice Frank and Fred's and Santa Fe Depot" is written on the back of this photo. The Red Cross, working with the National Guard and city police, responded and worked through the night to assisted in moving five hundred families in the path of the flood to Trinidad State Junior College and a Catholic community center, designated safe accommodations. The Red Cross arranged for seven tank trucks from the Pueblo Ordinance Depot to haul 3,590 gallons of water to Trinidad, and the Colorado State Hospital in Pueblo provided blankets and medication. *Photo courtesy of Faoro Family Photo Archives.*

A déjà vu view! The 1955 flood was captured rushing by the front of the Santa Fe Depot in Trinidad on May 17, 1955, by the Aultman studio. The structure in this photo was built following the 1904 flood, which left only one wall of the previous depot standing, and it was built to last. Despite the raging waters, the structure survived, and the greatest loss was in the basement, where items were stored. *Photo courtesy of History Colorado, Stephen H. Hart Research Center.*

WEDNESDAY, JUNE 16, 1965

36 hours of rain to the east and north "set off the worst floods in 30 years."

1.46 inches of rain fell on June 16, followed by another .96 of an inch reaching cloudburst intensity periodically on the 17th.

These sudden rains resulted in an 18-foot wall of water rushing down the Purgatoire through Trinidad driven by mountain rains that quickly filled all of the tributaries to the west.

More than 1,000 people had to leave their homes and seek refuge at Trinidad Junior College, assisted by the National Guard.

U.S. Highway 85 was washed out or submerged heading both north and south, cutting Trinidad and nearby communities off almost completely.

As it made its way into Trinidad, highway bridges providing access to the small towns were washed away. Phone lines were torn down by the powerful flow, interfering with communication. A telegraph operator at the Santa Fe Depot reported that he was trapped in the station with the water rushing through the depot rising to three feet. A spokesman for the Santa Fe Railway indicated that this flood was the worst since the flood of 1925.

Area railroad companies once again suffered the greatest losses, paralysing passenger service between Colorado and Kansas for weeks and leaving the Santa Fe station in Trinidad filled with up to four feet of silt in some areas.

On the industrial side, a C&W train making its way down the canyon with loaded coal cars fell into the Purgatoire just below Valdez when the saturated earth beneath the tracks gave way.[100]

After the significant damage of the 1955 flood, there was renewed interest in finding a permanent fix for the Purgatoire. In June 1955, the Purgatoire dam project, along with thirty-four other projects, was included in an omnibus flood control bill that was passed by Congress but vetoed by Persident Eisenhower. In February 1957, Representative James E. Donnelly of Colorado presented a memorial to Congress requesting the construction of the Purgatoire dam, and it passed unanimously. In 1958, President Eisenhower signed a rivers and harbors omnibus bill that approved the building of the dam, but funding still needed to be appropriated. The Army Corps of Engineers continued to plan for the project, but the initial allocation of funds to begin the project didn't come until April 1967.

A night to remember! Highway bridges were washed out, and the coal trains pulled fewer cars to lighten their loads, but the ground was so saturated that the tracks still gave way by Madrid, sending the engine into the river. Cars remained on the bank, providing a way to higher ground. "Fred Pedri was the engineer and Charlie Scaputti was on the caboose. Johnny Farrero was head brakeman, Mike Cuccia was front brakeman, and Weston Thomas was rear brakeman. Bob Scalko was the conductor" (interviews with Charles Martorano, C&W Railroad superintendent, and Mike Cuccia). *Photo courtesy of Steelworks Center of the West, Bessemer Historical Society, Pueblo, Colorado.*

In the meantime, the Purgatoire went on a rampage two more times—in May and June 1965—with a United Press story reporting that the May flood was the worst since 1925, according to a Santa Fe Railroad official. Highway bridges were washed out, and the coal trains pulled fewer cars to lighten their loads. The ground was so saturated that the tracks still gave way by Madrid, sending the engine into the river, but cars remained on the bank, providing a way to higher ground for the crew. Charles Martorano, the superintendent for the railroad, remembered,

> *Fred Pedri was the engineer and Charlie Scaputti was on the caboose.*
> *Johnny Farrero was head brakeman and Weston Thomas, Don Ferrero,*

and Bob Scalko were crew members. When they saw that the track was gone they jumped off of the engine and ran into a little barbed wire fence and got a little scraped up. . . . That was it. . . . Everything went okay. . . . They all survived, that was it. [101]

With help from the community, the channel of the river was altered to allow the engine to be raised. It was given a second life of service, restored by the local shop and repainted to become the "Patriot" for Colorado's centennial and the United States' bicentennial celebrations in 1976.

Chapter 3

J. EDGAR CHENOWETH
FINDS THE FUNDING

J. EDGAR CHENOWETH

J. Edgar Chenoweth was born in Trinidad in 1897 and grew up attending local schools and the University of Colorado. He was employed by several local companies as a young man, including the Colorado and Southern Railroad (C&S), Continental Oil Corporation and the Colorado Supply Company. He became a lawyer in 1925 and served as Trinidad's police magistrate for two years. He was appointed assistant district attorney for the third judicial district from 1929 to 1933 and county judge from 1933 to 1941. He was first elected to Congress in 1940, serving eleven terms between 1940 and 1965—having lost reelection during the Eighty-First Congress from 1950 to 1951.[102] He is credited with sponsoring the Fryingpan Arkansas project, which was designed to divert water from the Fryingpan River through the Rocky Mountains to the Arkansas Valley, supporting the Purgatoire River Dam in Las Animas County and bringing eight military sites to Colorado, including the Air Force Academy and Fort Carson.[103]

During Chenoweth's tenure in Congress, he testified many times regarding the devastation of the floods at Appropriations Committee hearings and was also involved with the Southeastern Colorado Water Conservancy District. At the Arkansas River Compact Administration's annual meeting on December 4, 1954, he was asked to talk about the history of the Purgatoire River Dam Project.

The project had been started some 20 years ago in somewhat different form. In about 1940 the Corps of Engineers had submitted an unfavorable report. This had been reviewed in 1942. In April 1942 a bad flood hit Trinidad and further study was made by the Corps of Engineers changing many items. This report was released in 1944.

In 1950 a meeting was held in Trinidad following which the present favorable report was made on a project involving some $17,000,000. This was put before Congress but not included in the Omnibus Bill of 1954 for several reasons, mainly due to lack of time for full step-by-step procedure. It was sent to the Bureau of the Budget in June 1954. There had been a Senate Hearing on it, but it had not been approved because it lacked approval by the Bureau of the Budget.[104]

Following the 1936 Flood Control Act that gave the Army Corps of Engineers the responsibility for managing rivers, a team of engineers visited the area to locate potential sites and returned to discuss their findings at a meeting in 1937. At that time, they had identified five potential sites: Long Canyon, Laurencito, Sarcillo, West Canyon and Burro Canyon.[105] In his closing remarks at the meeting, Congressman Chenoweth stated that he could ensure there would be continued efforts to fund the project when the next session convened.

Part of the concern with this new project stemmed from the recently completed John Martin Dam project. The path of the Purgatoire River eventually merges into the Arkansas River east of the town of Las Animas, approximately sixty-five miles from the Kansas border. The 1886 and 1925 floods had shown that a flooded Purgatoire not only impacted people and property along the river's banks, but it also sent surging waters into the Arkansas River, continuing the damage and stranding trains moving to and from Kansas City. In 1940, work began on the John Martin Dam and Reservoir on the Arkansas River in Bent County. Construction was suspended in 1943, during World War II, beginning again after the war and reaching completion in October 1946. That addressed concerns of those in Colorado and Kansas along the Arkansas River, but the 1942 flood was a reminder that a problem still existed on the Purgatoire.

FUNDING TIMELINE FOR THE PURGATOIRE RIVER DAM PROJECT

1937

A team of engineers visits Las Animas County to look at potential dam sites. A meeting the previous night included photos of the 1904 flood.[106]

1952

Representative J. Edgar Chenoweth announced that construction of a dam and reservoir, to be located west of Trinidad on the Purgatoire River, won preliminary recommendations by the Army Engineers.

The anticipated cost is 17 million dollars.[107]

1954

January 2—Army Engineers announce plans for a $17 million Colorado Flood Control Dam on the Purgatoire River near Trinidad.[108]

June 22—Former mayor James E. Donnelly and county commissioner John Kancilia urged the State Water Board to approve construction of the proposed $17 million flood control and reclamation project to be located above Trinidad on the Purgatoire River.

Right of way costs would be $2,004.00.

N.M. Gildersleeve, chief engineer for the Board, said that "water would be set aside for eventual use in developing synthetic fuel from coal."

Harold Christy, of CF&I in Pueblo, said that they would not file protest to the project, but would expect compensation for coal land lost through the project.

F.D. Everett, of the Federal Bureau of Mines, warned that seepage from the dam might extend one-and-a-half miles on each side—impacting 532 million tons of coal.[109]

October 27—The Arkansas River Compact Commission was unable to come up with a recommendation regarding the $17 million flood control and irrigation project above Trinidad on the Purgatoire River.

It was decided that further study was needed to determine to what extent the John Martin Dam water levels would be depleted if it is constructed—a concern to Kansas interests.

Ivan C. Crawford, director of the Colorado water board, anticipated that it would only be ³/₁₀ of 1% in an average year.[110]

1956

May 25—Purgatoire Flood Control Demand Being Renewed. After the May 19, 1955 flood Las Animas County was designated as a disaster area, making SBA loans available to businesses impacted.[111]

June 22—A House Public Works Subcommittee approved 34 flood control projects in various parts of the country including the dam on the Purgatoire River near Trinidad and recommended to the full Public Works Committee that the projects be included in an omnibus flood control bill that would be presented to Congress.[112]

1957

Representative Donnelly presented a memorial to Congress requesting the construction of a dam on the Purgatoire River above Trinidad to save the town from eventually being destroyed by repeated flooding of unusually high velocity.

The dam was initially part of an omnibus bill passed by Congress, but vetoed by Pres. Eisenhower. The memorial passed unanimously.[113]

1958

President Eisenhower signed an omnibus rivers and harbors bill that included the authorization for construction of the $17 million dam on the Purgatoire River above Trinidad.

The next action must be appropriation of funds.[114]

1961

Army Engineers recommended that Congress appropriate $200,000 for the next fiscal year to provide sufficient funding to provide advanced engineering and planning for Purgatoire River dam near Trinidad.[115]

1963

Members of the Colorado Conservation Board received information from the Omaha office of the Army Corps of Engineers that it is ready to begin construction of the project.

The project has been authorized by Congress, but funds have not yet been appropriated.[116]

Representative J. Edgar Chenoweth urges the House appropriations subcommittee to vote $1 million for the Purgatoire River water project....

"Chenoweth told the committee that Army engineers had almost completed planning for the Purgatoire River flood control and irrigation project in Trinidad."[117]

1964

J. Edgar Chenoweth urged a $1 million appropriation, within the budget that begins on July 1, for the Purgatoire River water project near Trinidad.

He stated that Army engineers have estimated that they would use $1.5 million during the year to begin construction and award an initial contract.

The total cost is now estimated at 20.8 million.[118]

1967

U.S. Army Corps of Engineers has been allocated the first $700,000, of the $22 million project, to begin land acquisition for the Purgatoire River dam and reservoir project.

U.S. Representative Frank Evans stated that this allocation insured the project's future.

It is estimated that the project will be completed in late 1972 or early 1973.[119]

Felix L. Sparks, president of the Colorado Water Conservation Board, spoke about the many water issues in the state, saying that attorney Saunders and Col. Hottenroth reported that the Trinidad Reservoir Project [was] *in "one of the happier situations in the state."*

This Bureau of Reclamation Project, estimated at $22 million, is due for a construction beginning date in the spring of 1968.

Land acquisition is expected to be completed in early "fiscal 1968," according to Hottenroth. "Every effort is being made to rush the Trinidad project and the only legal entanglement, since the repayment agreement was completed between Purgatoire River Water Conservancy District and the Bureau of Reclamation, is likely to center on land acquisition."

Representatives of the Real Estate Division (of the Bureau of Reclamation) visited Trinidad recently to update appraisals for the area which will be required for the construction of the outlet works.

"The District will determine whether or not condemnation in the U.S. Federal District Court of Colorado will be necessary to obtain the right of possession in order to allow activity on the initial contract for the 'outlet works.'"[120]

1968

Groundbreaking for the $25 million Trinidad Dam on the Purgatoire River is set for September 6, and it is anticipated that Floyd E. Dominy, U.S. Commissioner of Reclamation, and strong advocate for the project, will participate.

Work had actually begun several months earlier when a contract was awarded for dam outlet works.[121]

1973

Colorado Supreme Court rules against CF&I claim for retaining water rights of the Purgatoire, even though they had not used those rights for 54 years.

In 1918, CF&I built a central washery in Pueblo and phased out the smaller washeries, including the one in Sopris.

Because those rights remained idle, the water rights were deemed abandoned for an unreasonable amount of time.

They were returned to the Purgatoire River Water Conservancy District and the City of Trinidad with Rudolf Styduhar Jr. as the project engineer.[122]

PART IV

COMING TOGETHER
AS ONE COMMUNITY

While there were unique qualities within communities, and while families tended to settle near one another across generations—as children married and formed autonomous households—when you are a small community, it takes everyone playing a part to accomplish some things. People earned their living as miners or by providing services to miners and their families within the various neighborhoods, yet there are five areas that stand out in which residents from all neighborhoods came together to act as one community: work, worship, music, school and sports.

Chapter 1

WORK

Miners and their families faced an uncertain future each day, due to the occupational hazards of mining and dangerous conditions in the mines. As many accident reports recount, it could be the unintended act of one miner that led to the deaths and injuries of many. Sopris mines had fewer accidents than many nearby, but in May 1922, an explosion that claimed seventeen lives occurred. It was written up in the *Tenth Annual Report of the State Inspector of Coal Mines Colorado 1922.*

Each annual report covered one major explosion and looked at what the industry could learn from each accident that year.[123] Like other professions, mining is a brotherhood, and when a fellow miner needs assistance, all respond. Such was the case during the Dawson, New Mexico mine disaster on October 22, 1913, when 263 lives were lost. Nearby Colorado miners were on strike and in heated conflict with the management, but all put these issues aside as they made their way to Dawson to offer what assistance they could to their fellow miners.

Realizing the risk they took each day that they went into the mines, and understanding the hardship that injuries and deaths caused families, Italian miners in Sopris organized and chartered a fraternity to assist injured and out-of-work miners and to provide assistance to their families in the case of a miner's death. The Society of Mutual Benefit (Fratellanza Operaia di Mutuo Soccorso) was organized on the third day of January 1915 by about 140 Italian workers, in particular those from the province of Trento. It was unanimously approved that Sopris would be the society's location, as long as there were sufficient members to serve as officers and board members. The society was incorporated under Colorado law on March 22, 1923—just one year after the March 1922 accident—with the objective to "protect and help its members, and to render more friendly and brotherly relations between the Italians and those of the Province of Trento."[124]

Within the aforementioned "subsidies," members could be compensated for lost wages if struck by illness or accident (at a rate of seven dollars per week the first six months), and if hospitalization was required, the member was to select the nearest one and be accompanied by another member when going there. Additional "specifics" anticipate subsidies that would be given in the case of lost limbs, sight or hands and fingers, but we won't go into that. In the event of a miner's death, all members of that mining camp were required to attend the funeral, and seventy-five dollars would be given to cover expenses, plus one hundred dollars for death benefits.[125]

The members' handbook goes on to discuss specifics of many types, but the fundamental point was that the members were there for each other, and the families of members, in case no one else was. The society continued until the end of Sopris, and its property (lot 445 on block 14 of St. Thomas) was purchased by the Army Corps of Engineers in December 1968.[126] Meetings were also held at the Cunico store or the Brunelli store following church on Sunday, at least monthly.

A second society, Silvio Pellico Society, shared the space and was also compensated for the land in December 1968.

Beyond personal health and safety, when the local mines began to shut down between 1925 and 1935, not every miner had a car or a way to get to another mine, so they carpooled, and the riders paid a small amount each day to help with gasoline. Some went south to Morley and others west to the Frederick mine in Valdez and, eventually, the Allen mine.

Each mine throughout the state had at least one mine safety team and, often, a men's team and a women's team. All team members were trained in first aid and practiced procedures for assisting and evacuating injured miners, calling on a team member to play the part of the injured miner. The teams competed annually and were judged on how well they responded to a given situation. Qualifiers were invited to the state capitol to be recognized.

Beyond their dependence on each other in the mines, miners were there for each other and their fellow miners' families when faced with property

Societa Fratellanza Operaia di M. S DI SOPRIS, COLO.
Fraternity for a Better Society

PREAMBLE

The Italian workers and those of the Province of Trento, having arrived at Sopris, Colorado, and feeling the necessity of organizing a society of Mutual Benefits, on the 3rd day of January 1915, united in a number of about one hundred and forty (140) by unanimous vote deliberated: "This society bears the name of Fratellanza Operaia di Mutuo Soccorso, with its see at Sopris, Colo."

This society can remain at Sopris as long as there are sufficient members to direct the same. The object of the society is to protect and help its members, and to render more friendly and brotherly relations between the Italians and those of the Province of Trento.

Organized the 3rd day of January, 1915, and incorporated under the laws of the State of Colorado, on the 22nd day of March, 1923.

STATUTO FONDAMENTALE

DELLA

Societa' Fratellanza Operaia di M. S

DI SOPRIS, COLO.

LAS ANIMAS COUNTY,
U. S. OF A

La presente constituzione fu presentata in assemblea generale il giorno 18 Agosto 1935 e ne fu date lettura per tre riunioni generali, ed approvata il 20 ottobre 1935 Ed entratta in vigore il giorno 20 Ottobre 1935.

Top: Realizing the risk they took each day that they went into the mines and understanding the hardship that injuries and deaths caused families, Italian miners in Sopris organized and chartered a fraternity to provide financial assistance to injured and out-of-work miners. Additional support was provided to the family of any miner who died in the mines. The Society of Mutual Benefit (Fratellanza Operaia di Mutuo Soccorso) was organized on the third day of January 1915 by about 140 Italian workers, in particular those from the province of Trento. *Photo courtesy of Faoro Family Archives.*

FUNDAMENTAL STATUTE

OF THE

Societa' Fratellanza Operaia di M. S.

OF SOPRIS

LAS ANIMAS COUNTY, COLORADO,
U. S. A.

The present constitution was presented at the general assembly of the 18th day of August 1935, and was read at three general meetings. Was approved and went into effect on the 20th day of October 1935.

Bottom: Miners are a brotherhood of courageous men who go deep into the earth each day, never knowing if they will see the light of another day. In Sopris, they were not only coworkers but also multiple generations of families working side by side as fathers and sons or sons-in-law, cousins, brothers or uncles and nephews. When they worked, they worked hard, and when the work week ended, they gathered together to socialize. Their fraternities and lodges were built around their concern for each other and for each miner's family, as reflected in the organization's name and bylaws. *Photo courtesy of Faoro Family Archives.*

RITUAL

~•~

OF THE

SOCIETY

"Fratellanza Operaia"

OF

MUTUAL BENEFIT

~•~

SOPRIS, COLORADO

The Society of Mutual Benefit members' handbook goes into great deal to address potential situations and the role of the organization in helping members during those times. The society continued until the end of Sopris, and its property (lot 445 on block 14 of St. Thomas) was purchased by the Army Corps of Engineers in December 1968. In addition to their designated meeting place, monthly meetings were also held at the Cunico store or the Brunelli store following church on Sunday. *Photo courtesy of Faoro Family Archives.*

SOCI FONDATORI

Angelo D'Ambrogio	Domenico Praudi	Giovanni Colafrancesco	Pietro Salavatore
Andrea Stefan	Ernesto Lira	Ilario Batistella	Pietro Lira
Angelo Maset	Egidio Mosca	Luigi Montibeller	Pietro Belegante
Attilio Batistella	Francesco Brunelli	Lorenzo Terre	Pietro Oppio
Antonio Zotta	Francesco Leonetti	Luigi Muton	Rocco Soda
A. Zancanaro	Francesco Terre	Luigi Molinari	Rocco Segafreddo
Antonio Turra	Filippo Sartori	Luigi Mangiatore	Romano Belegrante
Antonio Daldegan	Francesco Belegante	Leone Lira	Raffaele Sartor
Andrea D'Angelis	Federico Turra	Luigi Celli	Romano Bassani
Angelo Garofali	Francesco Springhetti	Mario Gloder	Rocco D'Angelis
Antonio Vecellio	Filippo Zamparella	Massimo Covi	Salvatore Leonetti
Antonio Sella	Gaspare D'Ambrosio	Marco Finco	Saverio Coletti
Angelo Cunico	Giovanni Cerami	Marsango Gioacchino	Serafino Bonato
Angelo Faoro I.	Giuseppe Zaccaron	Marco Grando	Silvio Volpato
Angelo Faoro II.	Girolamo Lira	Martino Oppio	Teodosio Soda
Angelo Faoro III.	Giovanni Stefan	Mario Perin	Vitale Maninno
Antonio Faoro I.	Giovanni Batistella	Nicola Soda	Valentino Frigo
Augusto Vecellio	Giovanni Lira	Nicola Oppio	Vitto Giannari
Antonio Perin	Gervasio D'Angelis	Nardino Vittorio	Virginio Giannari
Andrea Vittorello	Giuseppe Leonetti	Olivo Zanotelli	alentino Maschio
Antonio Zamparella	Giuseppe Palombi	Pietro Daldegan	Valentino Martini
Antonio Pompele	Giovanni Sartori	Prospero Lira	Vincenzo Lauretti
Antonio Viecelli	Giuseppe Arboid		
Bortolo Stefan	Gio. Coletti		
Bernardo Lucia	Giacinto D'Ambrogio		
Bortolo Vecellio	Giuseppe Lucia I.		
Batista Padovan	Giuseppe Lucia II.		
Batista Zotta	Giovanni Grando		
Christiano Carli	Giovanni Faoro		
Cristiano Basso	Giuseppe Turra		
Catterino Basso	Giovanni Billesimo		
Celeste Munari	Giuseppe Faoro		
Cataldo Rossi	Giuseppe Bonato		
Domenico Bonato	Giuseppe Brunello		
Domenico D'Angelis I	Giacomo Deldosso		
Domenico Gasperetti	Giuseppe Massarese		
Davide Lira	Giacomo Pais		
Domenico Piffalo	Giuseppe Guercio		
Domenico Rosati			

28

29

Fratellanza Operaia di Mutuo Soccorso founding members. While dominated by men from the regions of northern Italy, this list includes the names of men from Sicily and throughout Italy, such as DeAngelis and Salvatore from near Rome and Terre and Cerame from Sicily, to note a few. *Photo courtesy of Faoro Family Archives.*

Having enough daylight for a photo at the end of a winter workday was a rare thing for these miners, who woke early and got home just before winter's dark crept in. Frank Noto married Mary Komora, who grew up next door to what became the Angelo and Jennie Faoro home. After marrying, Frank and Mary continued to reside in Sopris, so Frank and Angelo took turns driving to work—providing each other good company and help during the commute if the need arose. *Photo courtesy of Faoro Family Photo Archives.*

loss, most often due to fire. In an interview, John Sebben spoke of the night his family's home on Dexter Street caught fire and how neighbors rushed in to help save as much of the house's contents as possible. He specifically recalled seeing Angie Incitti hoisting his mother's cedar chest onto her back single-handedly and carrying it out to the street. Others were equally involved, but Angie's adrenaline rush was most memorable.[127]

Tano Zamborelli spoke of the New Year's Eve night that a chimney fire at the Regusa home spread to the house and, again, everyone nearby responded. The Colletti store was not in use, so the Regusas' belongings were taken there for safekeeping until the house was rebuilt. The next summer, when miners would have typically taken a vacation, many pitched in to rebuild the home.[128]

A similar story was repeated by Bob Cunico as he spoke of the fire that claimed the Yanes's home and tavern, remembering how others saved what

Above: The Sopris men's mine safety team was often in the top four at the regional competition level and one of the top teams in the state, which meant that they were often invited to the state capitol for recognition. In 1943, they brought home the green ribbon from the Fourth Annual Accident Prevention and First Aid Meet held in Denver on July 30 and 31. The members varied from year to year, and this particular year the team included (*left to right*): Frank Modica, August Zamborelli, Frank Noto, Angelo Faoro, Angelo Zancanaro, Gerald Sebben. Teams demonstrated their skills in first aid and mine rescue at annual competitions held by the Industrial Commission of Colorado. *Photo courtesy of Faoro Family Photo Archives.*

Opposite: Some went south, some went west; each one did what was best. When the Sopris mines closed down, miners were faced with deciding where they could complete their careers and earn their benefits. Some chose Morley, and others chose Valdez; eventually, they had no nearby choice other than the Allen Mine. As neighbors and friends, they took turns driving each other to work. *Back row, left to right*: Angelo Faoro, George Stakich, August Zamborelli. *Front row, left to right*: "Geronimo," Joe DellaBetta, Gerald Sebben. *Photo courtesy of Faoro Family Photo Archives.*

they could and helped sort through the cooled ashes for coins, jewelry and other things that might have survived. People rallied around the family, providing what was needed.[129]

In an interview, Charles (Chuck) Cambruzzi emphatically stated, "I learned to share!"[130] He has taken that "Sopris Spirit" with him throughout his life.

Chapter 2

WORSHIP

By 1911, St. Thomas Church was one of thirty-two camp churches that were "mission" churches served by the clergy of Holy Trinity Catholic Church in Trinidad. In the 1860s, as the land was being claimed following the Homestead Act, the Catholic Church saw the need for establishing a diocese in Colorado, since Colorado was currently under the oversight of Kansas. Bishop Miege made a trip from Leavenworth to this new area in the summer of 1860 and requested that the Catholics in Denver unite and build a church, promising to send leadership soon. He was able to have the Pike's Peak area transferred to the Santa Fe diocese, and Father Machebeuf was assigned to work in Colorado and Utah, Idaho and Montana. He arrived in Denver in October 1860, and from there, he and his assistant, Father John B. Raverdy, visited each mining camp within the assignment. On March 16, 1868, Father Machebeuf was appointed bishop and Father Munnecom was assigned to Trinidad.[131] An engraved stone remains in front of Most Holy Trinity Catholic Church acknowledging Bishop Machebeuf's role.

As mentioned previously, the church at Sopris was constructed on part of the five lots that Thomas Martin, a cofounder of St. Thomas, deeded to Father Charles M. Pinto in 1890. Rather than holding weekly Mass at each location, priests visited the churches on a rotating basis, taking care of the various sacraments during those times. For a period of time, Mass was said at St. Thomas only once each month.

May—the month of Mary—coincided with many events in the community, including baccalaureate for the graduating seniors. The boys are (*left to right*) Frank Concini, Anthony Vecellio and Leroy Long and the girls are (*left to right*) Konnie Brunelli, Shirley DellaBetta, Yvonne Sebben and Priscilla Arguello. *Photo courtesy of Faoro Family Photo Archives.*

As more priests were assigned to Las Animas and Huerfano Counties, they were able to bond more closely with the people of the parishes. Each brought his own special gift to the communities he served, and all were important, yet a few stand out in the memories of former residents. If there was an event in a town or in the county, they were likely invited to participate. In addition, with Most Holy Trinity Catholic Church being the priests' residence and the location of Holy Trinity School, additional interaction occurred. Those former Sopris residents still living fondly remember Father Joseph Haller as a friend of the community who loved to be among the people of Sopris. They fondly recall that after Sunday Mass, he would join the men at the bocce alleys of the taverns and then sit down with a family for Sunday dinner before heading back to the tavern. He was first assigned to the missions in Cokedale, Starkville, Morley, Tijeras and Sopris in 1937.

Beyond Father Haller's concern for people's spiritual needs, he was concerned for their everyday needs. In August 1940, he attended a session on credit unions while attending the Summer School of Catholic Actions in Denver. As he listened to the comparison of a credit union to a bank, he was led into thought regarding the poor in his parish and the loan sharks they were forced to turn to, since no other option existed. He believed a credit union could be a very beneficial thing in Trinidad and returned home to learn more about creating one. After speaking about the idea informally to many, a meeting was held at Holy Trinity, and formation of a credit union was approved. Officers were elected, and slowly but surely, the people began to take out and repay loans and learn financial management skills.[132]

Father Haller was a member of the county's child welfare committee and was also very interested in the Blue Cross's hospitalization insurance plans, often knowing parishioners who were in need of such care.[133]

During World War II, Father Haller was called up to fill the need for navy chaplains, serving in the Pacific Theater from 1943 to 1946, and returning to Trinidad in April 1946.[134] After Trinidad, he served in Pueblo, Wyoming, and then Kansas City.[135] He celebrated his diamond jubilee on August 7, 1982.

Father Fitzsimmons became the parish priest in the 1950s and was an integral part of the community and its events, attending school functions and saying the baccalaureate Mass for each graduating class. He was chaplain of the Newman Club at Trinidad State Junior College, and the students attending from Sopris and the other camp churches he had been assigned to were familiar faces as he met additional students from farther away. He acted as chaperone, and the group planned local outings and attended area conferences.

In July 1965, Father Paul Mendrick, a native Puebloan, was named pastor of Mt. Carmel Church in Trinidad.[136] He continued in that role as the dam and reservoir were funded and the rumor that had been out there for so many years became a reality: people would no longer be able to live in Sopris in the near future.

In 1968, Father Mendrick was assigned an assistant pastor, the recently ordained Father James Koenigsfeld, who had grown up in Iowa and was a young friend of Father Ervin Schmitt, a fellow Iowan who had come to the Diocese of Pueblo just after his ordination in 1958. Father Jim arrived in Colorado by July, and with Father Mendrick, they continued the traditions that had been established and kept the spirit of community alive.

"Father Jim" is the oldest of eleven children, and while he's not from a family of miners or mill workers, his family owned a small general store in Iowa, so he grew up in a small, close-knit community as well. Having young siblings, he easily related to the youth still remaining in Sopris, and he loved the out-of-doors, so he led hikes to the top of Fishers Peak occasionally. As of this writing, he is retired and living on the western side of the state, where

A Father and a friend, the Reverend Joseph Haller S.J. provided more than just spiritual guidance and is remembered by former residents as a friend of the community who loved to be among the people of Sopris. He was instrumental in establishing a local credit union for his congregation and served on the county's Child Welfare Committee. Joe Terry recounted a time when Father Haller—always able to enjoy a good joke—had parked in downtown Trinidad to run an errand before heading to the church, and when he got back into his car to leave the parking spot, the car started but would not move forward. Pranksters had inconspicuously jacked the car up just enough to prevent the tires from coming in contact with the pavement while Father was on his errand. *Photo courtesy of Christina Cunico Miller and Cunico Family Photo Archives.*

Father Fitzsimmons S.J. was not only the parish priest at St. Thomas Church in Sopris during the 1950s, but he also continued to work with many of the students as the chaplain of the Newman Club at Trinidad State Junior College. The girls of the class of 1954 asked to be photographed with him following their baccalaureate Mass. *Photo courtesy of Faoro Family Photo Archives.*

he still enjoys outdoor activities. He isn't Italian, but he is German, so the polka music played at gatherings and events, such as wedding receptions, is familiar to him. He has returned to the south shore of the reservoir for the past four Sopris Reunions, celebrating Mass in a "revival" tent, reviving the spirit and kinship of Sopris once again.

When the end had come and all land had been purchased, including the property the church was built on, Father Mendrick wrote a letter to the parishioners of St. Thomas, past and present, that said, in part:

> *I am sending this letter to you for several reasons. First of all, I want to thank you for your acceptance and cooperation with the Assistants of Mt. Carmel during these past nine years and for all the years before when the good Jesuit Fathers were your parish priests. The Mass at Sopris on July 4th was a beautiful tribute to the priests who served for all those years.*
>
> *Secondly, I am sure that Fr. Jim's departure from Trinidad was all the more difficult because of your love and respect for him, which was well deserved. I know this.*
>
> *In the third place, I want to let you know of the disposition of various things at Sopris. The government gave us $15,600.00 for the church, and we had to pay $212.50 for attorney's fees. The church bell will be mounted in front of Mt. Carmel church to the west side with a plaque specifying its origin. The organ will be brought to Mt. Carmel Church; the pews will probably be installed in the church at Cokedale; and the remaining moveable items will be given former parishioners. (Some have asked for things and offered donations for same....)*
>
> *Finally, I regret that very many of you had to move into the parishes where you could find homes. You know I admired and loved your spirit and wished that you all lived in Mt. Carmel parish, but know this, you are most welcome here at Mt. Carmel at any time. We will grow, I am sure, in the realization that we are God's people, and when we understand this in our hearts, we will have arrived at the perfect love.*

As mentioned previously, in addition to St. Thomas Catholic Church, a Methodist Episcopal church was located in Main Sopris on Wolcott Avenue near the entrance to Sopris Canyon and referenced as an attribute of Sopris in city directories.

Chapter 3

MUSIC

Did they bring their instruments across the ocean on the ships? Was there room for them? Their music would have made the journey more pleasant.

Whether their instruments came to the United States from their homelands or whether they were purchased on arrival, music was an important part of every community as a personal joy and as a member of bands and ensembles. Just after the turn of the century, each mining camp had a band that represented it and provided entertainment for the community. Paul Costa was the original band director, as indicated in city directories at the beginning of the twentieth century and just beyond, and in addition to the miners' band, there were community bands made up of anyone who wished to participate. Costa was also the owner of the International Theater in Sopris and provided the accompanying music needed for complete enjoyment of the silent films.

By the 1930s, Paul had passed the baton to his son-in-law, Virginio Fantin, who gave private music lessons on pretty much any instrument. Later, he was in charge of the school band, even though he lacked a teaching degree. In his book, *Legacy of an Italian Coal Miner*, Virginio's older son reflects on a Sunday afternoon progression of the band, stopping to play a few songs in each neighborhood and being rewarded with bottles of pop supplied by local store owners in appreciation. Virginio's youngest child graduated in 1943.

"That men who work long hours deep in the semi-darkness of coal mines…would choose to devote their leisure time…to the study and practice of music, may seem incredible…. Yet it is true that in the camps and plants of the Colorado Fuel and Iron Company and the Rocky Mountain Coal and Iron Company there is musical talent of a high order among the men" (*Camp and Plant*, January 16, 1904). Sopris was one of those camps with many talented musicians, and many of them came together in the fall of 1903 to establish a camp band, directed by Paul Costa. Perhaps they played a Sunday afternoon concert in St. Thomas Church before taking this photo next to the church. *Photo courtesy of Duane Zanotelli.*

Above: When Paul Costa chose to no longer lead the Sopris band, Virginio Fantin filled those shoes and gave private music lessons to many in the community as well. *Top row, left to right*: Minnie Machone, John Coszalter, Dan Archuleta, Joe Antista, Paul Fantin, Tony DeAngelis, Kelly Vecellio. *Middle row, left to right*: Sentino Coszalter, Jane Zancanaro, Joe Sebben, Wayne Savio, Mary Jeanette DalDegan, Bobby Kancilia. *Front row, left to right*: Frank Cerame, Ernest Lira, Billy Huxby, Mike Zucca, Virginio Fantin (bandleader), Willy Salvatore, Angelo Zancanaro, Ermen Lira, Sam Incitti, Frank Martini, Sam Antista, Jasper Butero, Erminio DeAngelis, Louis Fantin. *Photo courtesy of Ruth Berry Wilson & Fantin Family Photo Archives.*

Opposite, bottom: Paul Costa came to the United States from Palazzo Adriano on the island of Sicily to work in the mines in 1898. His wife, Lena, and son, Charles, joined him the following year, and two daughters and another son were born in the United States. Paul soon became involved with the local band and was given the role of leader, and by 1915, he and Victor Peccaro owned the International Theatre in Sopris. Paul provided the musical accompaniment for the silent films by playing a piano during the movies. *Photo courtesy of Ruth Berry Wilson and Fantin Family Photo Archives.*

By the 1950s, a certified music teacher, Ernie Montoya, was in charge of the band, and class was held in the gym across the street from Lincoln School. Montoya's day began in Sopris; then he drove to Hoehne and on to Branson for his final classes, each day.[137] Joyce Lira was a student teacher in Sopris before relocating.[138]

John Cunico was just a few years shy of being able to graduate from high school in Sopris, but he remembers attending basketball games while there and how the lights would go dark for halftime and each band member's hat had a small light that they turned on while performing precision drills as they played their instruments and moved into various configurations with the lights creating the letter *S* or an image.[139]

In addition to the school music program, there was no shortage of bands and ensembles in the area. School dances and sock hops were popular, wedding receptions and anniversary celebrations were frequent and area dance halls provided live music each Saturday night. In the 1926 *Nuz-Heep*, the school newspaper, the "Christmas Wishes" section reported that "Rose Mazzarise wants more Saturdays in a week to go to more dances." Piedmont Tavern was a popular local venue, and Mary Ida Buccola Oliver stated that her family often went to Starkville on a Saturday night.

George Kelloff had a five-piece orchestra that played on weekends and also for school dances, as publicized in the school newspaper in 1955.

Many of the children in Sopris learned to play the accordion, and for most, it was a fun skill. There were a few who played professionally, including

George Kelloff and his orchestra were well known throughout the mining communities. As a student at Trinidad State Junior College, Kelloff was an active part of the school band and was part of a touring group that went to local high schools to perform and create interest in TSJC's music program. He played at local high school events, and his orchestra performed at TSJC's Engineers' Ball, where everyone was said to have had a wonderful time. He married Edna Mae Cunico, daughter of Pena and Crist Cunico. *Photo courtesy of Kelloff Family Photo Archives.*

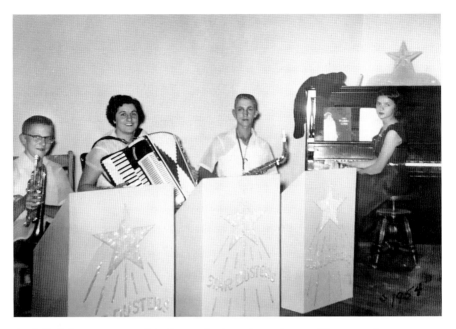

Angie Incitti was an accomplished accordionist and was always willing to get the younger generation involved in music, forming this band and recruiting choir members for the church choir. Joyce Lira (*at the piano*) recalls, "From left to right, it was Victor Macchietto (trumpet), Angie Cunico (accordion), James Bonato (saxophone), Joyce Lira (piano). We also had a drummer, who is not pictured. Our original drummer was Pat Tapia, and then later, Kirby Bonato played drums with us….This picture was taken at the Piedmont Tavern dance hall during a practice session." *Photo courtesy of Joyce Lira Anderson Photo Archives.*

George Zanotelli Jr. Joe Incitti taught himself to play the accordion, and his daughter, Angie, became proficient as well. She would play solo at events and gatherings but also had a small band known as the Star Dusters that played in nearby towns, as well as Sopris, in the 1940s and 1950s. Several young musicians were given opportunities to be part of the ensemble.

As TV came into the community and everyone could not only hear the music but also see the bands, more "garage" bands sprang up, with drummers and guitars instead of woodwinds and piano. One such band was the MGMs: Bernard Martorano, Gilbert Garcia and Jimmy Martinez. They weren't just a "garage" band. Bernard's cousin Diana remembers them setting up in the middle of the road to entertain the neighbors on summer days as the residents, young and not-so-young, formed a conga line weaving through neighborhood houses and yards—going in front doors and out back doors gathering participants as they went from home to home, with parents watching the fun and sometimes joining in.

Handsome enough to have a contract with MGM, the MGMs were Bernard **M**artorano, Gilbert **G**arcia and Jimmy **M**artinez. They came from different neighborhoods in Sopris and graduated from Lincoln High School in 1961, 1964 and 1962, respectively, when chart toppers were Elvis Presley, Bobby Vinton, Ricky Nelson and Dion to mention a few. *Photo courtesy of Gilbert Garcia Martinez Photo Archives.*

Even though not everyone belonged to a band, many played instruments and sometimes showcased their talents on the spur of the moment, like Paul Shablo, who happened to be available to join the Bill Thompson band for a number. *Photo courtesy of Shablo Family Photo Archives.*

With the popularity of so many who played the guitar on TV, many played independently, without belonging to a band but being able to sub in on occasion. Paul Shablo was one such musician; Paul Mondragon was another.

The school had a choir some years, and St. Thomas Church always had a choir that sang at Mass. It was predominantly made up of girls who attended St. Thomas Church, and Angie Cunico and LoRetta Archuletta and others accompanied the choir on the piano. When kids hit double-digit ages, the boys' rite of passage was to become altar boys and the girls became part of the choir.

Chapter 4

SCHOOL

As previously mentioned, the school was the major employer of local residents. In the early years—the first two decades of the twentieth century and before—women who taught were single, and if they married, a replacement was found. Tano Zamborelli remembered that in order to provide lodging for these single women, the community had a house with several bedrooms, called the teachery, where the women lived together. It was located near the school on Dexter Street, west of James Avenue. As the teachers had come from college dormitories, it was a reasonable accommodation.

Many who taught were alumni who had left the community to earn their teaching certification and then returned. Within the Deldosso family, Francis Deldosso taught art and was in charge of the seventh grade, according to the December 1926 *Nuz-Heep*. His sister, Dorothy, followed the same path and taught first grade for many years.

A second family with many teachers was the Benedetti family of Jerryville. Their second son, Mario, returned to Sopris to teach art and manual arts, including woodworking. He was also responsible for the ninth grade class and coached basketball and baseball. His younger brother John also returned to Sopris to teach, and he realized his ability to be a role model as a male faculty member. He began a young men's club that he named the Secret Service Club, with objectives that included building bonds across the grades and participating in social outings. On occasion, they would identify a way

Children from the various neighborhoods attended Lincoln School in Sopris and became lifelong friends. Dorothy Deldosso grew up in Sopris, the daughter of mine superintendent Jack Deldosso, and returned to teach the next generation of eager learners after earning her teaching degree. Those children identified by classmates and friends are as follows. *Back row, left to right*: unidentified, Antoinette Falduto, Mary Rose Antista, Mary Bellegante, JoAnn Buccola, unidentified, Norine Concini. *Front row, left to right*: unidentified, Domenic Antista, Joe Cuccia, unidentified, unidentified. *Photo courtesy of Robert Cuccia and Cuccia Family Photo Archives.*

to be of service and help in some way. They were required to wear a tie to each meeting, with whatever they were wearing, and since many families chose durable overalls for all the men of the family, that combination was very common. Irma, just two years older than John, did not teach at Lincoln School in Sopris but in a nearby school instead.

Between 1920 and 1950, members of the following families were listed in the census reports as residing with their parent(s) in Sopris and teaching in nearby public schools: Archuleta, Benedetti, Brunelli, Buccola, Cordova, Deldosso, Furia, Martini, Meneghini, Skidmore, Viccelli and Yanes.[140] By the 1950s, additional names included Faoro, Incitti and Sebben. Nick Furia did not teach for the local school district; he became an instructor in the building trades program at Trinidad State Junior College. Knowing that the

Ties were required for meetings of the Secret Service Club, John Benedetti's version of today's Key Club, and anyone was welcome to join. Sam Incitti remembers it as being more of an adventure club, going on outings to Long's Canyon. *Front row, left to right*: Sam Incitti, Tony Cambruzzi, Mike Mendoza, Victor Amador. *Middle row, left to right*: Mike Moquez, Anthony Faoro, Henry Rodighiero, Ernest Passero. *Back row, left to right*: Richard Skufca, John Benedetti, Vince Alishio, Tano Zamborelli. *Photo courtesy of Faoro Family Photo Archives.*

dam would be coming in a few years, Nick built his home so that it could be moved to Trinidad when the time came.

In addition to faculty members, there was a need for classified staff members, and both Mary and Angelo Zancanaro were employed at the school: Mary was in food service and Angelo was a janitor. Angelo also taught manual arts when there was a shortage of teachers who had those skills; he was referred to as "Maestro" by many students because he was a master craftsman. As their children graduated and moved on, the staff sometimes did also, creating a need for additional people to fill the positions; as a result, Jennie Faoro and Annie Macchietto worked in food service during the last years of the school.

When Gene McGinn took over as the principal for Lincoln School, he needed a new secretary. He asked around, and many people gave him Dora Faldutto's name. McGinn was able to find her at a baseball game, and he spoke to her about how highly she had been recommended and asked if she would consider being the school secretary. At the time, she was employed at

They called Angelo Zancanaro "Maestro" because he was a master of many trades, including woodworking, so he stepped in to teach industrial arts when the need arose. The Zancanaro home was filled with evidence of his talent: turned wood lamps, bookends, hand-carved animals and more. Any child wishing to know how could learn to make a whistle from a young branch with only a pocket knife. *Photo courtesy of Shirley Compton and Zancanaro Family Photo Archives.*

the sewing factory in Trinidad, so returning to Sopris where she would be with the people who knew her and who she grew up with was very appealing. When the Sopris school closed, her skills were well known and respected, and she was offered a position in the Trinidad school administration office.[141]

Just as some influenced by returning to teach, others influenced by going into other professions. Sixth graders at the Sopris school wrote their autobiographies for an assignment in April 1954. Tommy Zamborelli's mentions that he wants to go to college and be an electrical engineer, while Billy Brunelli's says he wants to work in radio and television. Elizabeth Antista credits Mr. FitzSimmons with such aspirations, because as principal, he introduced courses in drafting and related fields into the curriculum. As a result of his efforts, this new generation saw what was possible when older friends came home to visit. Bart Antista, Paul Fantin and Alfred Laiminger (graduates in 1943–46) became engineers and went on to work for airplane manufacturers—Bart's career was with North American Aviation, while Alfred and Paul were employed by Boeing.[142]

Chapter 5

SPORTS

BASEBALL

Many sports provide enjoyment, camaraderie and the ability to work together; baseball played an important role in developing those skills and more. People knew about baseball before coming to the United States, and once they were here, it was a source of Sunday relaxation, as player or observer. An official Las Animas County League was established in April 1913:

> *The Las Animas county baseball league with eight strong semi-professional clubs was organized last night at a meeting held at the offices of the Trinidad Electric Transmission Railway & Gas company. Representatives of local and camp teams were present, there being twenty-five enthusiastic baseball fans in attendance. The teams that will comprise the league are Cokedale, Starkville, Sopris, Aguilar, Hastings, Forbes, Bowen and the Power company team. H.J. Wightman, secretary of the Power company, was elected president of the league; H.H. Buob, of Cokedale, vice president; and H.J. Reid, secretary and treasurer.*
>
> *It was decided that a member of each team make up the executive board and draw up by-laws....Each team will be required to put up a stipulated guarantee to finish the season. It was not definitely decided what prizes would be offered for winning teams....*
>
> *The organization of a camp league was considered with a good deal of enthusiasm. The camps have gathered fast aggregations....It is probable*

that a post season series of games…between the county league and the Trinidad city league…[will] *be played during the county fair.*[143]

Mine teams did form, and how well you could swing a bat became as important as how well you could swing a pick—sometimes more so. Men were offered jobs at specific mines based on their athletic abilities, as much as—or more than—for their mining skills. Joe Martorano ("Martarano" in local papers) was a renowned baseball player, in part because of his batting. He was recruited by the Colorado Fuel and Iron mine in Valdez.

On Sunday afternoon, families would pack a picnic and head to the ballpark for the games. When the time came for Valdez to play Sopris, the game pitted Joe against his brother-in-law, Albert Macchietto, as pitcher for the Sopris team and his friend Metro Morgan who was the first baseman. Joe was not greeted warmly, since he was considered a traitor to his hometown.[144] The Komora brothers were often on the Morely team after the Sopris mines closed.

In *Coal Ball,* author Tim Dodson comes to this conclusion:

> *Due to the unique aspects in which the coal industry in southeastern Colorado formed and grew in the early twentieth century, baseball served not only as a social and communal outlet for the miners but as a way in which these miners developed a connection with their company and, in many cases, their new country. Taking up "America's game" not only showed their commitment to the country that provided them employment opportunity but made life easier in coping with the daily stresses associated with such a dangerous profession.*[145]

Because baseball requires limited equipment, and because both teams do not need the same equipment at the same time, it is possible to play the game among friends with just enough gloves for the fielding teams and a small selection of bats for the batting team, plus an open space free of large rocks or botanical intrusions. As a result, kids residing in Piedmont, St. Thomas and Jerryville often played in the street or on empty lots around town, while those in Main Sopris gathered at the school playground or the baseball field northwest of the gymnasium that began behind the Incitti home and extended west for two blocks and north toward the river. Players began at early ages, coached and assisted by older players, building very competitive teams as the years went by. The 1926 school newspaper, the *Nuz-Heep,* reported, "The grade boys easily won the county title, coming through the season without a defeat." Members of the boys' team included Louis Carazza, Joe Butero, Nello Phillips, Mike Crappa, Ernest Lira, Barney Brunelli, Nellie Tozzi, Jasper Picinato, Louis Yanes, Gendo Sebben, Petro Andregith (Andregetti), Joe Ameralli, Pete Ferri and Sam Guercia (Garcia).

Because Sopris players had so many years of playing together, when they entered into American Legion baseball in Trinidad, rules were made that prevented any team from having more than four players from Sopris on it at one time.[146] It was common for five or more Sopris players to make the all-star team each year. Chuck Cambruzzi recalls:

> *I played baseball for American Legion and we had one of the better teams in Colorado. If we would have won our last game, up in Greeley, we would have went to the World Series for that age group. We played together so much, even though there wasn't very many of us, we would go to Trinidad every summer and we were unbeatable because we played together for so much. They tried to recruit us to go to Trinidad High School, they asked Ernie Lira, myself, Kirby Bonato, and Eddie Stadjuhar to go to Trinidad High School to play sports and the only one that accepted was Eddie Stadjuhar.*[147]

Sopris high school teams were very competitive, and in 1944, they were undefeated, beating Hoehne 18–1 and 13–3 and Primero 13–6. John Benedetti was a faculty member and their coach until he was drafted and sent to Fort Warren in Wyoming for the duration of his service. He was often written up in the base newspaper, the *Fort Warren Sentinel*, for his baseball talents, earning the nickname Blasting Benny from fellow player, and later commentator, Kurt Gowdy. One article stated:

> *Most valuable man at the plate for Ft. Warren this year has been Sgt. John Benedetti. He ranked third in his batting percentage as June began, with .353 in eight games, but his leadership on extra base hits stamped him as the No. 1 slugger. Benedetti had 12 hits, more than any other player. He scored six runs himself, as many as anybody else. He led in runs batted in with 12, in home runs with three, and tied for most doubles with two….*
>
> *The lad from Trinidad, Colo., has come thru with long drives when men on base would bring in crucial runs….Built for power, with 182 pounds on a 6 foot 1 inch frame…now 27 years old, he has had eight years of*

The high school teams were very competitive, with coaches like Joe Martorano and John Benedetti, renowned home run hitters. Many of the boys played on American Legion Baseball teams in Trinidad, and several made the All-Star team each year. Members of the 1949 team were (*back row, left to right*) Paul Fantin, Joe Martorano, "Pap" George Sp___, John Maccagnon, Sam Incitti, Domenic Incitti, Joe Cassa; (*front row, left to right*) George Cassa, Crist Cunico, Tony DeAngelis, Bob Kancilia, George Butero, Joe Maccagnon, John Coszalter, Charles Mandrill. *Photo courtesy of Christna Cunico Miller and Cunico Family Photo Archives.*

experience from 1935–1942 with the Trinidad Red Sox, in 1943 with two Ft. Warren league teams....Benny has played everywhere on a ball team except behind the bat. His regular spot is center field.[148]

In the 1920s, girls played baseball as well, building their teams from both high school and grade school girls. The December 1926 *Nuz-Heep* reports that the high school girls' "team looked like champions and played like champions. Not only did the Sopris girls look good with their black and orange suits, but they seemed to know what it was all about."

The article goes on to identify the ten players—five from the high school and five from the grade school:

Rose Terry, captain and left field; Clara Alishio, catcher; Gladys McGuire, pitcher; Sylvia Daily, first base; Marie Yanes, second base; Violet Zanotelli, third base; Carmella Collovini, right field; Carolina Lira, centerfield; Annie Brunelli, right field; Rose Ferrero, first base and right field; Teresa Collovini, second base and centerfield; Gusta Brunelli, fielder; Angilena Mandrill, right short.

They played seven games and lost only one:

Sopris 61; Aguilar 7 (at Aguilar)
Sopris 54; Aguilar 5 (at Sopris)
Sopris 18; Primero 7 (at Primero)
Sopris 23; Primero 45 (at Sopris)
Sopris 25; Primero 10 (at Cokedale) [possibly the opponent was Cokedale]
Sopris 41; Hoehne 13 (at Hoehne)
Sopris 49; Hoehne 17 (at Sopris)

In addition to the school team, young women played on teams sponsored by local businesses and took on opponents as far away as Pueblo. Carrie Passero played for the Trinidad Motor Hub team, along with other area girls Alice Floyd, Caroline Matkovitch and Margaret McKenzie.[149] Carrie was a home run hitter and also had an excellent throwing arm that served her well into adulthood, as her children can verify.

BASKETBALL

Basketball followed baseball in importance and participation, with girls again having competitive teams in the 1920s and 1930s. To have a player taller than 5'10" was unusual, so being fast was more important than being tall. Each year's season ended with a tournament hosted by Trinidad State Junior College and opportunities to go on to district and statewide competitions based on the outcome. In addition, each participating high school selected a female student as tournament princess to represent their school, and she was considered for the title of "Queen of the Invitational Tournament." Cheerleaders also competed for a title, and one school received a sportsmanship award.

Bounding to a win! The YMCA Clubhouse served the community from 1916 until the mid-1950s. Crist Cunico was known for his athleticism. Determination like that depicted in this photo is a reason he was consistently the highest-scoring player in basketball games, sometimes scoring half of the team's points, closely followed by Domenic Incitti and John Sebben. In his childhood diary, Crist wrote that he had always wanted to play basketball and finally got the chance on February 9, 1945, against Weston. He acknowledged being scared, but over the next five years, he honed his skills. *Photo courtesy of Christina Cunico Miller and Cunico Family Photo Archives.*

A unified effort began as basketball teams made up of students from both St. Thomas School and Lincoln School met at the clubhouse to become a basketball team. *Top row, left to right*: Coach Sagath, Frank Shablo, Michael Tamburelli, Robert Zamborelli, Raymond Garcia, Roger Brunelli, James Bonato. *Bottom row, left to right*: Robert Leonetti, Tommy Niccoli, Michael Butero, Vic Macchietto, George Zanotelli, Tommy Martinez, Ray Barela. *Photo courtesy of Faoro Family Photo Archives.*

Coach Lois Palmquist was unique among men's basketball coaches in 1944. With most male faculty members serving in the military during World War II, there was a notable lack of coaches, so Lois Palmquist stepped up to coach the Sopris men's basketball team during the 1944 season. He husband, Dutch, coached for Trinidad, so he would sometimes attend practice and help a bit. Since Trinidad was in a different league, there was no conflict of interest. Pictured is the Sopris men's basketball team during the 1944 season. *Back row, left to right*: Lois Palmquist, Anthony Faoro, Bill Martini, Tony Cambruzzi, Alfred Laiminger, Bart Antista. *Front row, left to right*: Sam Incitti, Mike Mendosa, Angelo Incitti, Bill Archuleta, Tano Zamborelli. *Photo courtesy of Faoro Family Photo Archives.*

Initially, Sopris teams played at the YMCA Clubhouse, until the new gymnasium was built across from Lincoln school in 1953. Coaches for the men's team were not often mentioned in news articles, so it is more difficult to identify them, but it seems that Mr. Lawrence was the coach in 1925 and 1926 for both the boys' team and the girls' team. In the 1930s, Harold Threlkeld and Ragnar Edquist were coaches. By the 1950s, Mr. Sagath was coaching the grade school team, and high school coaches included Martin Anzellini, Mario Benedetti, Murray Franciscato and John Sebben.

Because so many men were called to serve during World War II in the mid-1940s, Lois Palmquist stepped up to coach the men's team during the 1944 season. Her husband, Dutch, coached for Trinidad, so he would sometimes attend practice as well. Trinidad was in a different league, so there was no conflict of interest. The team took second place in the county tournament and third place in the district tournament.[150]

As Chuck Cambruzzi remembers:

> *We were always good, but we just quite couldn't get there. We always went to Alamosa for our tournaments and everything, for some reason we always either won consolation or third prize—we never could get to that top rung….I can remember our senior [year], our tallest guy was Edwin Baca and he was 5 foot 9, and that was our center, so we were lacking in that, but we were good though, for our size we were good.[151]*

The 1955 team "swept the tournament in all categories," as the write-up in their "Senior Edition" of the school paper tells:

> *Yes, this was an exciting night as everyone was wondering whose school princess would be crowned queen of the tournament. Everyone held their breath while Mr. Baird announced that Isabelle Vigil, a member of the senior class at Sopris, was to be crowned queen.*

Tournament time! Each year, Trinidad State Junior College sponsored a county-wide basketball tournament, and each team chose a senior girl to be their queen candidate. In 1955, Sopris's candidate, Isabelle Vigil, was crowned tournament queen, and the other girls in this photo (*left to right*: Yvonne Sebben, Shirley DellaBetta and Mary Jane Incitti) won the cheerleading trophy. The guys came away with the junior championship trophy. *Back row, left to right*: Angelo Vecellio, Pat Tapia, Charles Gomez, Frank Concini. *Front row, left to right*: Manuel Ramirez, Anthony Vecellio, Bernie Morgan, Leroy Long, Tony Mincic. *Photo courtesy of Bernie Morgan.*

The Sopris students thought the excitement would never end for next came the announcement that the little lassies from Sopris had won the cheerleading trophy. Tears of happiness ran down the faces of these three senior girls as they ran out to receive their trophy from [their] fourth cheerleader and queen.

It looked like a small class reunion when five senior boys came onto the floor to receive the junior championship trophy. This night will never be forgotten because it meant so much to these senior students.

In 1925, the Sopris girls won the grade school championship, and many of the same young women were part of the 1928 county championship team.

The Sopris girls' team won the 1925 grade school championship and looked forward to the 1926 season, as the school newspaper from December 1926 reports. "The girls who played on last year's team are: Rose Mazzarise, forward and captain, Nellie Picinato, center, Carolina Mandrill, center, Rose Terry, guard, Sylvia Daily, guard, and Bronwen Davies, guard. These girls will be the ones around which Coach Robinson will build his team." *Front row, left to right*: ____, ____, Mary Mazzarise, Rose Terry (Sebben), Rose Mazzarise. *Back row, left to right*: Sylvia Daily, ____, ____, Coach Robinson, ____, ____. Unnamed members of the basketball team may include Clara Alishio, Gladys McGuire, Marie Yanes, Violet Zanotelli, Carmella Collovini, Carolina Lira, Annie Brunelli, Rose Ferrero, Teresa Collovini, Gusta Brunelli or Angilena Mandrill. *Photo courtesy of Frank Jerant and Mazzarise Family Photo Archives.*

Victory! Coach Harold Threlkeld began his teaching and coaching career at Lincoln High School in Sopris in 1927 after graduating from Colorado Teachers College in Greeley. After three years, he was promoted to superintendent but not before hiring James Reiva, a fellow Colorado Teachers College alum, to coach for him and continue his winning streak. *Front row, left to right*: Annette Rodighiero, Lena Concini, Marie Yanes, Erma Benedetti, Ida Terry, Charlotte Brunelli. *Back row, left to right*: Dora Meneghini, Ann Meneghini, Dora Ferri, Florence Wilson, Valerie Tatar. Superintendent Harold Threlkeld; coach James Reiva. *Photo courtesy of Ruth Berry Wilson, Robert Butero, and Michelle Sebben Sebastiani.*

In the 1930s, the Sopris girls were repeat local champions and played in the state tournaments. The 1935 team finished their season with only one loss to Primero and lost to them again in the early rounds of the tournament. The *Greeley Daily Tribune* noted, "Coach R.O. Edquist will unquestionably start his customary line-up with Miss Rhodighiero at center, Miss Yanes and Doris Meneghini as forwards and the guards picked from Julia Cunico, Teresa and Carrie Passero, and Louise Ferri."[152]

FOOTBALL

Football was seldom played at the high school level because of the varying availability of boys within classes and the overall size of the school. For example, the class of '43 had two boys, the class of '44 had three and the class of '45 had six. There was a football team in the 1950s for two years,

There were enough male students to make a football team only during 1956–57 and 1957–58, and they wore hand-me-down uniforms from a nearby mining camp. Goalposts were never erected, and Coach Sebben remembered that they could not even afford the chalk to mark the field. By the 1958–59 school year, the students had been redistributed to balance all county schools, and Sopris no longer had enough boys to make a team. *Back row, left to right*: Coach John Sebben Jr., Gene Vigil, Filbert LaCrue, Kirby Bonato, Fred Roybal, Joe Terry, Eloy Arguello, Leroy Espinoza, Ernie Lira, Chuck Cambruzzi, Coach Francescato. *Front row, left to right*: Gary Archuleta, Gary Terry, Camel Shablo, Bob Leonetti, Mike Butero, Al Shablo, Joskie Baca, Ron Sebben. *Equipment managers*: Possibly Joe DeAngelis and Nathan Lira. *Photo courtesy of Chuck Cambruzzi Photo Archives.*

then enrollment of boys dropped to the point where there were not enough players to make a team. The Sopris school also served students from Jansen and Cokedale and, later, Primero when it closed its school. The attendance boundaries were a bit flexible, allowing the county superintendent to shift students from one school to another to balance out class size and attendance. Chuck Cambruzzi believes there was a boundary change that relocated former players to other schools, making it impossible for Sopris to have a team the third year. Football was played at Trinidad State Junior College, and even though they lacked high school experience, several Sopris graduates became football players at TSJC, including Ted Langowski, Frank Martini and Jasper Butero Sr.

TRACK

While Sopris had a baseball field and a gymnasium for basketball, it lacked a track. The baseball field was large enough to be a practice field, and it was smoothed out for baseball games by dragging a heavy piece of wood behind a truck to even out the ridges and fill in the ruts.

In 1938, Trinidad State Junior College sent several freshmen to the state track meet in May; they represented the school well. Those who placed included Butero, Benedetti, Martini, Freyta, Moya, Stadjuhar, Pitt, Louden, Spradling, Strader, Sanky, Cany and Clay. In running, Trinidad took second in the mile relay, while Moya took first in the mile run, followed by Freyta in third. R. Pitt and Louden placed fourth and fifth in the 120-yard dash. Trinidad dominated the 880-yard run, when Moya came in first with a time of 2 minutes 9.4 seconds, and Spradling, Strader and Benedetti came in third through fifth. Butero took fourth in the broad jump.[153]

Track was not a thing at the high school level—just an occasional get-together with a nearby school arranged by Mr. Benedetti—but it was a thing at Trinidad State Junior College, and many from Sopris participated. Jasper Butero was not only a fast runner but also placed in discus, shot put and javelin. *Photo courtesy of Robert Butero and Butero Family Photo Archives.*

Equally strong in stationary events, Butero took first in discus with a throw of 114 feet, followed by Benedetti in third place and Martini in fifth. Shot put was won by a Colorado College student, and Trinidad—Butero, Volpe, Benedetti and Stadjuhar in that order—swept the rest of the places. In the javelin, Sanky, Butero and Cany took second through fourth.[154]

Because it took every boy to make a team for all sports, the boys were in shape, and the games they played in their leisure time often involved running and climbing, so putting those muscles to use for track came naturally. When John Benedetti returned to Sopris after college, he brought back skills and knowledge that included track technique and how to begin a race in a starting block stance. To give his athletes opportunities to practice these new skills, he collaborated with his friend and fellow alumnus Harry Raye— grandson of Teresa Bianchi and son of Rose—who was teaching at nearby Cokedale. The two of them set up track meets to allow their students to have that experience. In his book *Legacy of an Italian Coal Miner*, Louis Fantin reminisces about the first such track meet:

> *Sam Incitti and Ernie Passero were the stars of our track team and Richard Strock was Harry Raye's star. Strock didn't know the proper approach procedure that we had been taught by Benedetti…palms outstretched, measure two hand lengths from the center, lean forward one knee on the ground and push out with cleats when the gun goes off.…Richard just stood at the line with tennis shoes, no cleats…commenting to our members, "We never had no track training." What I didn't realize was how fast he was. He didn't need no track training.…After Cokedale we would refer to Strock as Richard Streak.*[155]

Joe Incitti came to the United States from Italy in 2013. He brought his Old Country work ethic and values with him and did not understand this new concept of sports in the schools, thinking it was time spent frivolously. As a result, his oldest son, Sam, found it necessary to have friends and teammates bring his shoes and uniform to events so he would not be in trouble with his father if he should discover them. When it came to track, Sam was outstanding—so much so that, at the annual county track meet his senior year, "Sam captured individual honors with his 36-point performance. He captured five first place ribbons, two seconds and one third for his totals for the day." As a result, Sopris ran away with first place, since Sam had earned more points that the rest of the team combined. The next nearest competitor was a boy from Thatcher whose individual score was 21.[156]

Sam was eventually found out, and his father began to understand how his children contributed to each team's success. He was won over and then faithfully attended the athletic events of Sam's four brothers. His second son, Domenic, was also a runner but not a sprinter. Domenic ran the two-mile run for Trinidad State Junior College, along with his lifelong neighbor and friend John Sebben. They, and all runners, were called cindermen because they ran on a track covered with cinders.[157]

GOLF

Even though there was never a golf course in Sopris, or a golf team, many residents went on to take up the sport after leaving. Many have golfed together for years; it is their way of staying in touch and keeping up with each other on a weekly or monthly basis. As of this writing, Sam Incitti is still golfing twice a week at age ninety-seven. Gary Archuleta and Robert (Doc) Leonetti organize an informal golf scramble in Trinidad on the Friday morning before the Sopris Reunion, which usually takes places every five years. Both men and women are welcome to participate in the golf scramble, and it is well attended, giving classmates a chance to meet the husbands of the girls they grew up with and the wives of the guys.

Chapter 6

A FINAL FAREWELL

NEW SOPRIS INC.

Emigration from Sopris began during the Great Depression, a few families at a time, and it accelerated as the mines closed and more people experienced life beyond Sopris, whether through military service or college. Colorado's Front Range also continued to develop. Some families left when they could not find work locally, or the father left and the wife and children remained at home and in school, and several were able to move back as the Allen Mine opened or other opportunities became available. Everyone was to depart after December 31, 1970.

While it was difficult for the men to leave and find new jobs at older ages, the need to take on a new mortgage—since the amount they were paid for their Sopris homes was far below current housing market prices—forced them to seek new employment. They had long since lost the GI Bill advantages that got many people into their first homes in the larger cities, so options were somewhat limited.

Leaving the neighborhoods and friends they had known for so much of their lives was also hard for the women. At first, being in the home with small children in a new country was somewhat isolating, but as the children grew up and the women had more free time and more opportunities to gather, they formed strong bonds. The women were going to miss this closely woven community of family and friends, and it was a deep sorrow that they felt.

Several men in the community saw this and sought to open options beyond buying a nearby home or moving to wherever their adult children now lived. They were hoping to find a way to keep the Sopris residents together, even though it would need to be on new land. A small corporation named New Sopris Inc. was created on July 24, 1968, as a "Colorado Corporation Nonprofit" with "perpetual existence." Its stated purpose was

> *to promote the building of a housing project in the County of Las Animas, State of Colorado to re-locate the residents of the Sopris, Piedmont and adjoining vicinity who are being forced to move from their present homes because of the construction of the Purgatoire dam project; and to acquire by purchase, gift, donations, or demise, and to hold for the purpose hereinafter mentioned, real estate in or as additions to City of Trinidad or within the County of Las Animas, and to lay out and plat the same into streets, alleys and blocks, and to sell and dispose of the lots and blocks so surveyed, laid out and platted, for the purpose of providing for building sites for the members of this corporation.*
>
> *The address of its initial registered office shall be 210 First National Bank Building, Trinidad, Colorado, 81082, Las Animas County. The name of its initial registered agent at such address is Harry R. Sayer.*

Five names are given as the "initial board of directors who shall serve until their successors are chosen": John Maccagnan, Crist Cunico, Louis Cunico, Jasper Butero Sr. and Richard Morgan. Harry R. Sayer was the notary public who signed off on the document.[158] The vision did not fully materialize, but many families were able to find homes near each other in Trinidad neighborhoods.

THE HONORABLE CONGRESSMAN FRANK E. EVANS

The plight of the people of Sopris was also taken up by Congressman Frank E. Evans when he addressed the House Committee on Public Works, Subcommittee on Roads on June 15, 1972. Before the process of purchasing land ended, the allocations for displaced homeowners changed with passage of Public Law 91-646, which gave those who had not agreed to sell their land to the U.S. government by early 1971 an additional allowance of up to $15,000 for their homes. During his remarks, Evans made several statements regarding the purchase of the land for the dam and reservoir and encouraged the committee to extend the additional relocation benefits to those who signed their documents prior to the December 31, 1970 deadline:

Sopris was a little town back in the mountains of the South-Central part of the state. It once was something of a mining center but that activity has declined. Most of the people who remained there were elderly, former miners or the descendants of miners.

Almost all of the 215 families that previously lived there had moved [before passage of the additional allowance], *receiving payments for their homes and property and such meager relocation assistance as was available under the law. On average they received between $4,500 and $5,000 for their homes. Those who qualified for any relocation aid at all generally got $400....*

In the case of Sopris we're not talking about wealthy people trying to pry a few more dollars out of the federal treasury. We're talking about a few small businesses and about 215 homeowners, most of them elderly, who had the misfortune of living in the way of a needed federal project.

Those who had been living in marginal or sub-standard housing had a definite problem.... The money they received for their home was not enough to begin to find safe, decent and sanitary housing so, in effect, they were driven from one sub-standard dwelling to another.

Savings were eaten up in some cases. Persons nearing retirement or already retired now face new home mortgage payments with very limited incomes. In short, the dislocation brought hardship to numerous families that could have been eased under the new law.

Evans went on to discuss some of the cases that had been settled and the additional amounts these families received, pointing out that refusing to honor the December 31 deadline had not been a cause for sanctions but, rather, led to significant advantages. He concluded with this statement: "I believe the present situation as I have described it represents an inequity that the Congress can and should remedy."[159]

FATHER JIM RALLIES THE FAMILIES

Having arrived as the process of dislocation was taking place, Father Jim quickly realized the love of the people for this small town. Rather than let it fizzle out, he rallied those families remaining, living and working nearby, to celebrate the town by inviting all former residents "home" for one last community event. This became the first Sopris Reunion, held on July 4, 1970. The day began with a Mass at the small St. Thomas Church, so well attended that the crowds overflowed into the parking lot. It was celebrated by several former priests.

From the Mass, people returned to the area by the school or their "old" neighborhoods to be with family and friends as they enjoyed picnic lunches. Because they had until December 1970 to move out, many homes were still occupied. The afternoon was filled with games and competitions, and in the evening, a dance was held in the gym, with music flowing into the street.

After the 1970 reunion, LoRetta Archuleta and Mary Jane Incitti, assisted by others nearby, picked up the torch and organized additional reunions that took place on the south shore of the reservoir where homes had been. People continued to flock to the shore to renew friendships and get to know the next generations of the families. As of this writing, the most recent Sopris Reunion was held on July 1 and 2, 2022, with over 250 people in attendance.

While the town is gone, the community remains, in new neighborhoods and supported through new organizations such as the Trinidad Historical Society in Trinidad and the Friends of Historical Trinidad in Denver. Anyone with a shared heritage or interest in the area is welcome to join the groups.

Fifty-two years after the first Sopris Reunion that Father Jim inspired, he joined former Sopris residents and their descendants once again for the welcome on Friday night at the amphitheater of Trinidad Lake State Park. Many who returned were junior high– and high school–age youth when attending the first reunion. Two more generations have come to know about Sopris through their parents and grandparents, and those who attended the first reunion continue to look forward to the chance to be with friends and family as everyone comes together approximately every five years and to welcome Father Jim back as their pastor for the weekend. *Photo courtesy of Mike and TommiRenae Brunelli Family Photo Archives.*

La fine di Sopris.

Povero Sopris le finito.
Sotto L'acqua vien Seppellito
tutti i tuoi Cari Amici
vencono a darti L'ultimo Addio,

noi Lasciami delle Rose
che Sotto Acqua tu Riposo
noi Beviami dele vino
che il tuo Nome e Sempre vivo.

per rigordo moi lasciami
sü di quella Montagnina
le tre lettere che vedeti
L. H. S. Restera

Above: The sight of "LHS" greeted the Incitti family as they opened the front door each day to head to work or school, and it watched over the small town constantly. The letters representing Lincoln High School remain on the hillside to the south of the neighborhoods, although they're currently overgrown and faded. When Sopris was inhabited, that hillside was just challenging enough to make it fun to climb and just high enough to put our lives in perspective as we looked down on our community. It was where the large TV antenna was mounted when television entered our lives, and it was where UFOs took off from during the 1960s. It was probably where Joe Incitti harvested wood for the family's forno, which kept the letters visible. As former residents, we hope that those letters will be allowed to remain highly visible on that hillside to forever remind us that we once lived there and to let others know that as well. *Poem courtesy of the Pikes Peak Library District Special Collections, Colorado Springs, Colorado.*

Opposite: Giuseppe (Joe) Incitti arrived in the United States in 1913 and eventually made his way to Sopris. His need for shoe repair brought him to the Randisi Shoe Repair shop in Trinidad, where he met Jennie, the owner's niece. They married within the year, and together, they raised seven intelligent, athletic and talented children, two daughters and five sons: Angie, Sam, Domenic, Guerrino (Corky), Angelo, Mary Jane and Joseph. *Photo courtesy of Monique Hartman and Incitti Family Photo Archives.*

THE END OF SOPRIS

BY JOE INCITTI

Consider the town of Sopris finished.
It will be buried under water
But today all friends will come together
For last looks and last goodbyes

We will leave all the roses
To rest beneath the water
But we will drink all the wine
While the name of Sopris lives forever.

In order to remember we will leave
Upon that little mountain
These three letters that you see
L.H.S. (Lincoln High School)

Appendix A

PLAT MAPS

SAINT THOMAS PLAT MAP

The mines preceded the "official" neighborhoods, even though people had settled in the area by the 1860s. Saint Thomas, Main Sopris and Farrelville were surveyed and plats created in 1888 and 1889. The areas were eventually under CF&I ownership but began as part of the Denver Fuel Company, whose mission statement was (in part) "to acquire purchase, own, hold, work, lease, and sell coal lands and other lands in the State of Colorado and elsewhere; to prospect for, develop, mine, and sell coal and other minerals… and in general to do any and all the aforesaid and such other things as to promote the general purposes of such corporation, or [that] may be necessary or proper in the successful transaction of its business."

As the Colorado Fuel Company and the Colorado Coal and Iron Company merged to become Colorado Fuel and Iron in October 1892, they bought the lands of the Denver Fuel Company and other lands during the process. The newly formed company opened up opportunities in the long run that allowed the miners of Sopris to continue career paths at nearby mines when the Sopris mines closed down.

The plat for St. Thomas was filed and recorded on May 12, 1888, signed by Thomas Martin and George W. Thompson (a.k.a. G.W. Thompson). Both men had been in the area since the 1800s. Thompson was involved in mining with Horace Long under the name Raton Coal and Coke Co. at a town named Thompson that was located in Long Canyon with access to the Denver Texas & Ft. Worth Railroad.

38

State of Colorado ss. I hereby certify that the above and foregoing is a true and correct copy of the original instrument of writing filed for record in my office at 4 P.M. May 12th A.D. 1885.

Jesus M. Garcia
Recorder
By Eugene Garcia
Deputy

Know all men by these presents that Thomas Martin and George W. Thompson have laid out and sub-divided into lots and blocks to be known as "St. Thomas" a certain tract of land, as shown by the annexed plat, and situated in the S½ of SE¼ Section 28 Township 13 S. Ro. 61 W., in Las Animas County, State of Colorado, and the streets and alleys as shown by said plat are dedicated to public use

Thomas Martin
Gr. W. Thompson

State of Colorado
County of Las Animas

Seal

I John W. Doublet a Notary Public in and for said County and State, Certify that Thomas Martin and George W. Thompson, personally known to me to be the persons whose names are subscribed to the above instrument of writing, appeared before me and acknowledged the execution of the same, for the purposes therein set forth this 5th day of July 1890.

"My Commission expires Sept 11 1890"

John W. Doublet
Notary Public

State of Colorado
County of Las Animas

I hereby certify that the above and foregoing was entered on the book July 18 A.D. 1890 at 11 o'clock P.M.

Jesus Ma Garcia. Recorder
By Eugene Garcia. Deputy

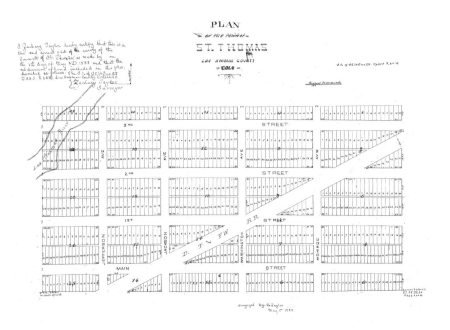

Saint Thomas plat map. *Courtesy of Las Animas County.*

SOPRIS PLAT MAP

Supported by the research of Greg Everhart, USACE archaeologist, the first Sopris mine opened in 1887, and early photos of Main Sopris include the Colorado Supply Company Store (see page 57) and small homesteads. Other houses existed near the mine entrance in Sopris Canyon and on other land owned by the mines and leased to the workers so that they could built their own lodging (see Little Italy on page 37). The official plat of Main Sopris was filed and recorded on February 26, 1889, signed by W.H. James, vice president of the Denver Fuel Company.

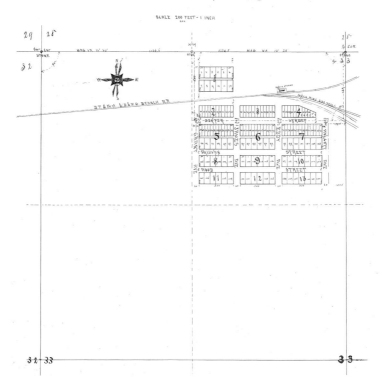

This page and following: Sopris plat map. *Courtesy of Las Animas County.*

54

Know all men by these presents: That The Denver Fuel Company a corporation, has laid out and subdivided into lots and blocks to be known as the Town of Sopris, a certain tract of land, as shown by the annexed plat, and situated in the N.E¼ of N.W¼ of Sec 33. in Tp 33. S of R 64 W. in Las Animas County, Colorado, and the streets avenues and alleys as shown by said plat are dedicated to public use, as such, subject to the reserved right of said Company and its assigns to lay gas and water-pipes therein: to erect telegraph and telephone and electric light poles, plant trees and irrigate the same, therein, and to build railways therein, or permit the same to be done. Provided, also that in case any street, alley or avenue, or any part thereof, be vacated or ceases to be used as such the title thereto shall thereupon revert to said company or its assigns. Lengths, widths and distances are indicated on the plat in feet and tenths of feet.

That portion or tract of land lying between Blocks 1 and 2. and that north of Blocks 2 and 4, and occupied by railway tracks and station house as well as all other portions not specifically included within lots, alleys and named streets and avenues are not dedicated to public use, but all rights therein are expressly reserved by and to said Company, and its assigns.

In testimony whereof the said Company has caused these presents to be signed by its vice president (its president being absent) and attested by its Secretary and Corporate Seal, at Denver, Colorado, this 20th day of February, 1889

The Denver Fuel Company
By W. H. James
Vice President

Attest D. C. Beaman,
Secretary

Co Seal

State of Colorado } ss.
County of Arapahoe }

I, Maurice S. Donnelly a Notary Public in and for said County, hereby certify that on this day before me personally came W. H. James to me personally known to be the person who signed the foregoing instrument as Vice President of the Denver Fuel Company, and acknowledged the execution of the same to be the voluntary act and deed of said Company, by him as vice President voluntarily done and executed for the uses therein specified.

Witness my hand and seal this 23. day of February, 1889

Seal

Maurice S. Donnelly, Notary Public

State of Colorado } ss.
Las Animas County }

I hereby certify that the above and foregoing is a true and correct copy of the original Plat and writings thereof filed for record on the 26 day of Feby. 1889. at 9 o'clock A.M.

Jesus Maldonado
Recorder
By Eugenio Garcia
Deputy

FARRLVILLE PLAT

The plat for Farrlville (a.k.a. Farrelleville and Farrellville) was filed and recorded on August 17, 1888, but no owner or company appear on the historical document, so as of this writing, it is unclear why the community was named Farrlville and who hired Fred N. Archibald to prepare the plat.

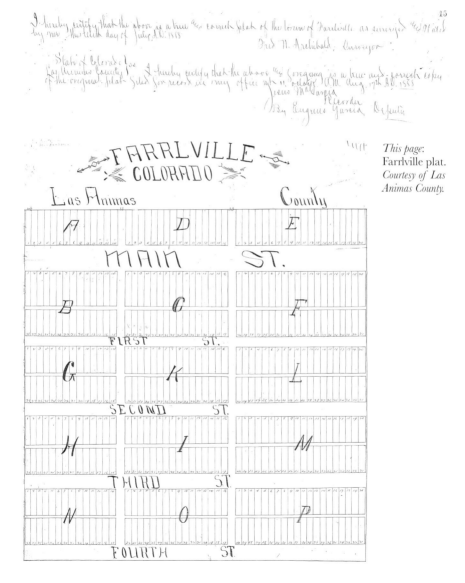

This page: Farrlville plat. *Courtesy of Las Animas County.*

FINAL LAND BUYOUT

BETWEEN 1968 AND 1970

It was said that Jack Shields and his team began farthest east at Piedmont and worked their way west. Jack E. Shields was appointed as the project manager, while John R. Cobb signed the sale contracts as chief of the Real Estate Division from the Albuquerque District Corps of Engineers.

For the sake of following the path of reported purchases, the maps below start at the far east and move to the west.

The maps are available courtesy of the USACE Albuquerque District Office and with the authorization and collaboration of Kim Falen, operations project manager of Trinidad Lake, and Danielle Galloway, supervisory biologist and chief of the Environmental Resources Section of the U.S. Army Corps of Engineers, Albuquerque District.

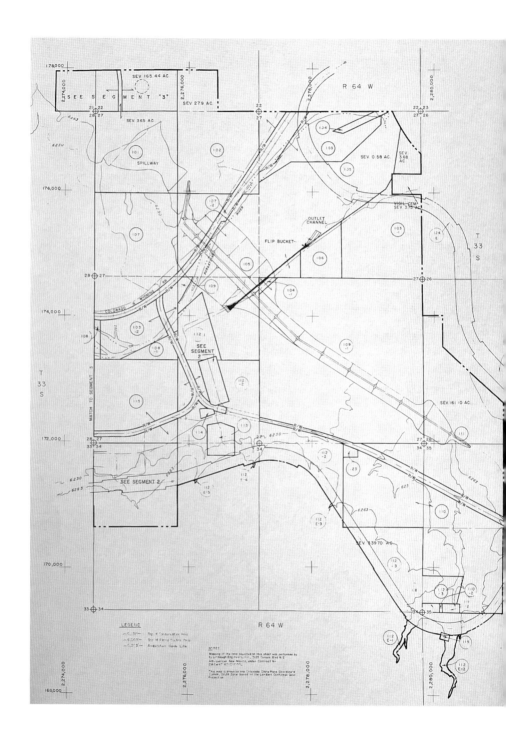

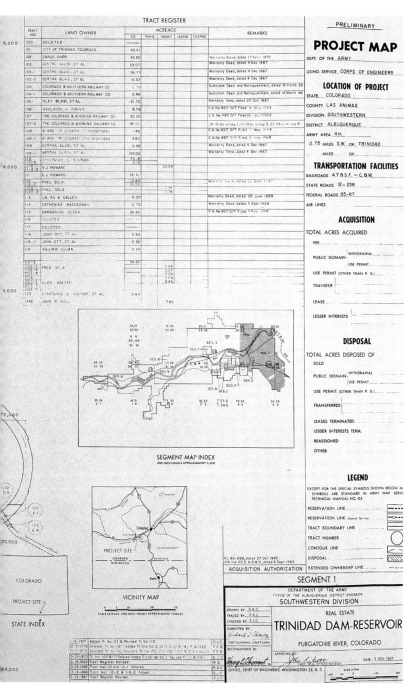

Easternmost landowners.

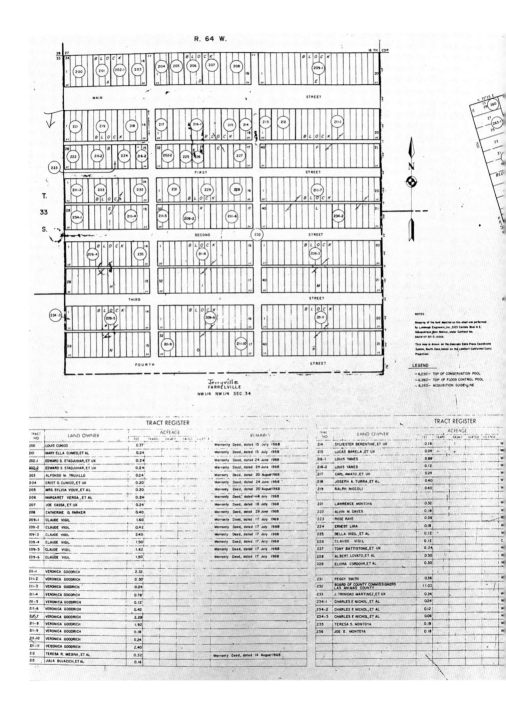

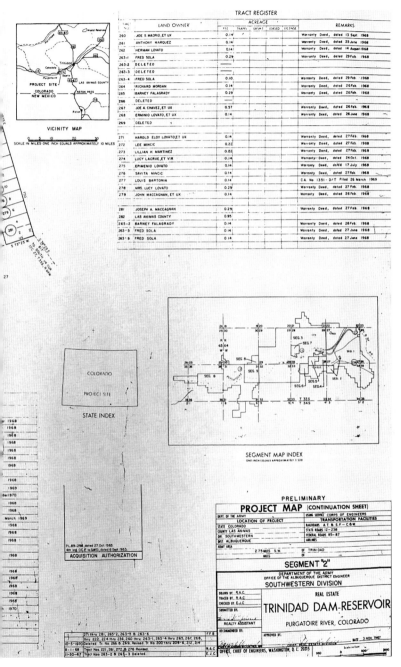

Piedmont and Farrlville (Jerryville) overview.

177

TRACT REGISTER

TRACT	LAND OWNER	ACREAGE					REMARKS
		FEE	TRANS.	EASM'T	LEASED	LICENSE	
260	JOE S. MADRID, ET UX	0.14					Warranty Deed, dated 13 Sept. 1968
261	ANTHONY MARQUEZ	0.14					Warranty Deed, dated 25 June 1968
262	HERMAN LOVATO	0.14					Warranty Deed, dated 14 August 1968
263-1	FRED SOLA	0.29					Warranty Deed, dated 29 Feb. 1968
263-2	DELETED						
263-3	DELETED						
263-4	FRED SOLA	0.10					Warranty Deed, dated 29 Feb. 1968
264	RICHARD MORGAN	0.14					Warranty Deed, dated 26 Feb. 1968
265	BARNEY FALAGRADY	0.29					Warranty Deed, dated 26 Feb. 1968
266	DELETED						
267	JOE A. CHAVEZ, ET UX	0.57					Warranty Deed, dated 26 Feb. 1968
268	ERMINIO LOVATO, ET UX	0.14					Warranty Deed, dated 26 June 1968
269	DELETED						
271	HAROLD ELOY LOVATO, ET UX	0.14					Warranty Deed, dated 27 Feb. 1968
272	LEE MINCIC	0.22					Warranty Deed, dated 27 Feb. 1968
273	LILLIAN H. MARTINEZ	0.22					Warranty Deed, dated 26 Feb. 1968
274	LUCY LACRUE, ET VIR	0.14					Warranty Deed, dated 24 Oct. 1968
275	EPIMENIO LOVATO	0.14					Warranty Deed, dated 17 July 1968
276	SAVITA MINCIC	0.14					Warranty Deed, dated 27 Feb. 1968
277	LOUIS BARTONIA	0.14					C.A. No. 1351- D/T Filed 26 March 1969
278	MRS. LUCY LOVATO	0.29					Warranty Deed, dated 27 Feb. 1968
279	JOHN MACCAGNAN, ET UX	0.14					Warranty Deed, dated 26 Feb. 1968
281	JOSEPH A. MACCAGNAN	0.29					Warranty Deed, dated 27 Feb. 1968
282	LAS ANIMAS COUNTY	0.95					Warranty Deed, dated 26 Feb. 1968
263-2	BARNEY FALAGRADY	0.14					Warranty Deed, dated 27 June 1968
263-5	FRED SOLA	0.14					Warranty Deed, dated 26 Feb. 1968
263-6	FRED SOLA	0.14					Warranty Deed, dated 27 June 1968

VICINITY MAP

SCALE IN MILES: ONE INCH EQUALS APPROXIMATELY 10 MILES

PROJECT SITE
COLORADO
NEW MEXICO

PIEDMONT
PART OF E1/2 SE1/4 SEC. 27

Piedmont tract register.

178

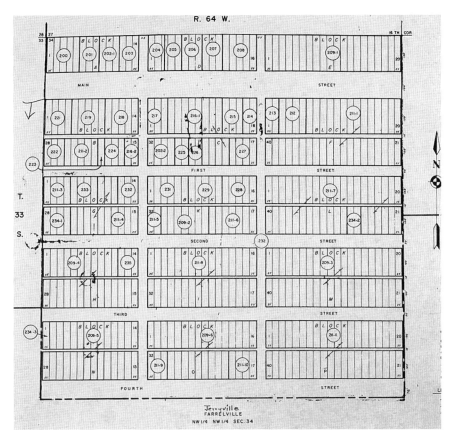

Farrelville.

Farrelville tract register.

179

APPENDIX B

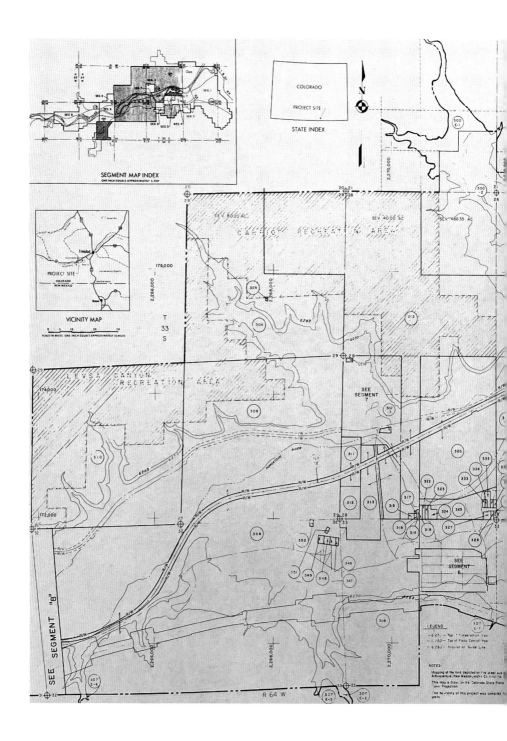

180

TRACT REGISTER

TRACT NO	LAND OWNER	FEE	TRANS	EASM'T	LICENSE	PERMIT	REMARKS
300-1	CHARLES D. CHOATE	29.09					
		102.50					
300E-1	CHARLES D. CHOATE			17.05			
300E-2	CHARLES D. CHOATE			2.29			
301	PAULINE L. IRONS	80.00					
302-C	FRANK CUCCIA, ET UX	0.63					C.A. No. 1773, date of Final Judgment
302-1		240.82					Warranty Deed, dated 27 April 1970
302-2	FRANK CUCCIA, ET UX	4.66					Warranty Deed, dated 27 April 1970
302-3		0.32					Warranty Deed, dated 18 Oct. 1969
303-C	TRUSTEES OF SAN ANTONIO RELIGIOUS ORGANIZATION	0.85					C.A. No. 1773, date of Final Judgment
304-C	SAMUEL LOVATO AND CARPIO MARTINEZ TRUSTEE FOR NEW CARPIO CEMETERY	0.71					C.A. No. 1773, date of Final Judgment
305	VERONICA GOODRICH	0.04					
306	RUDY SANTISTEVAN, ET UX	115.96					Warranty Deed, dated 18 March 1970
307-1	THE C.F.& I. STEEL CORPORATION	14.07					
307-2		15.26					
308	ROSE SEBBEN, ET AL	517.43					
309-1	DELETED	—					
309-2	DELETED	—					
300E-3	CHARLES D. CHOATE			0.37			
300E-4				0.18			
310	THE C.F.& I. STEEL CORPORATION	160.00					
311	A.D. LOUDEN	5.17					C.A. No. 2357, D/T Filed 15 June 1970
312	ROSE RAYE	4.00					Warranty Deed, dated 22 Dec. 1970
313	HOWARD K. THOMPSON, ET UX	19.30					Warranty Deed, dated 18 Dec. 1969
315	ANNA AND TONY RAMIREZ	0.21					Warranty Deed, dated 19 May 1969
316	M.E. FURU	0.09					Warranty Deed, dated 10 July 1970
317	MANUEL M. MEDINA	0.04					C.A. No. 2357, D/T Filed 15 June 1970
318	VERONICA GOODRICH	0.16					
319	FRANK J. GONZALES	0.24					Warranty Deed, dated 7 July 1970
321	DELETED						
322	MARGARITO AND CLOTILDA SANCHEZ	0.26					Warranty Deed, dated 16 March 1970
323	ANTHONY RAMIREZ	0.26					Warranty Deed, dated 18 March 1970
324	FRANK J. GONZALES	0.64					Warranty Deed, dated 23 June 1965
325	FRED BACA, ET UX	9.34					Warranty Deed, dated 20 May 1970
326	ANGELO BLASI, ET UX	65.11					Warranty Deed, dated 27 April 1970
327	ROCCO DeANGELIS	0.39					Warranty Deed, dated 11 Dec. 1961
329	ROCCO DeANGELIS	0.17					Warranty Deed, dated 27 April 1970
331	SEBASTIANA AGUALLO	0.17					
333	GEORGE ZANOTELLI, ET UX	0.14					Warranty Deed, dated 10 Feb. 1969
334	JOE DELLA BITTA, ET UX	0.14					Warranty Deed, dated 15 May 1969
335	PETE BACA, ET UX	0.46					Warranty Deed, dated 10 Feb. 1969
336	MARIE OPHELIA LOVATO	0.13					Warranty Deed, dated 31 Oct. 1968
337	ROSE SEBBEN	0.17					Warranty Deed, dated 23 June 1969
338-1	BERT CHAFLIN	0.57					C.A. No. 2357, D/T Filed 15 June 1970
338-2	BERT CHAFLIN	5.70					C.A. No. 2357, D/T Filed 15 June 1970
339-1		1.02					Warranty Deed, dated 27 April 1970
339-2	CANDIDO MARTINEZ	0.60					Warranty Deed, dated 27 April 1970
339-3		1.53					Warranty Deed, dated 27 April 1970
307E-1	THE C.F.& I. STEEL CORPORATION			2.66			
307E-2				0.88			
341	JOHN W. LANGOWSKI	10.74					Warranty Deed, dated 7 July 1970
342	JOSEFITA TRUJILLO, ET AL	2.62					
343	CARLOS LONG, ET AL	5.71					Warranty Deed, dated 18 Dec. 1969
344	SAMUEL LOVATO	1.58					Warranty Deed, dated 12 Dec. 1968
307E-3	THE C.F.& I. STEEL CORPORATION			0.18			
346	ALFRED SANTISTEVAN	0.15					Warranty Deed, dated 7 July 1970
347	JIM TRUJILLO	0.39					Warranty Deed, dated 3 June 1969
348	RUTH MEDRANO	0.30					Warranty Deed, dated 12 June 1969
349	VERONICA GOODRICH	0.30					
307E-4	THE C.F.& I. STEEL CORPORATION			3.35			
307E-5				0.02			
351	THE FURU REALTY AND INVESTMENT CO.	0.11					Warranty Deed, dated 10 July 1970
352	VERONICA GOODRICH	0.13					
307E-6				0.33			
307E-7	THE C.F.& I. STEEL CORPORATION			0.10			
307E-8				0.04			
307E-9				0.10			

PROJECT MAP (CONTINUATION SHEET)

DEPT. OF THE ARMY		USING SERVICE CORPS OF ENGINEERS	
LOCATION OF PROJECT		TRANSPORTATION FACILITIES	
STATE	COLORADO	RAILROADS	A.T.& S.F. — C.& W.
COUNTY	LAS ANIMAS	STATE ROADS	12 - 239
NR.	SOUTHWESTERN	FEDERAL ROADS	85 - 87
DIST.	ALBUQUERQUE	AIRLINES	
ARMY AREA			
	2.75 MILES S.W. OF TRINIDAD		
	MILES		

SEGMENT 3

ACQUISITION AUTHORIZATION

PL. 89-298, dated 27 Oct. 1965.
4th Ind. OCE to S.W.D. dated 6 Sept. 1963.

DEPARTMENT OF THE ARMY
OFFICE OF THE ALBUQUERQUE DISTRICT ENGINEER
SOUTHWESTERN DIVISION

REAL ESTATE

TRINIDAD DAM-RESERVOIR

PURGATOIRE RIVER, COLORADO

OFFICE, CHIEF OF ENGINEERS, WASHINGTON, D.C. 20315

DATE 12 JULY 1966

SHEET 3 OF 9

What is now Carpios Recreation Area and Levsa Canyon Recreation Area and the area south of the river.

INSET No. 1

64 W

SEE INSET No. 1

TRACT NO.	LAND OWNER	ACREAGE FEE	EASM'T	REMARKS
400	BARBARA GOMEZ LOVATO	0.15		Warranty Deed, dtd 31 Oct 1968
401	RACHAEL VECELLIO	0.07		Warranty Deed, dtd 18 July 1968
402	MADELINE VECELLIO	0.37		Warranty Deed, dtd 17 July 1968
403-1	VERONICA GOODRICH	0.64		
403-2	VERONICA GOODRICH	0.15		
403-3	VERONICA GOODRICH	1.7		
403-4	VERONICA GOODRICH	0.09		
403-5	VERONICA GOODRICH	1.58		
403-6	VERONICA GOODRICH	0.33		
403-7	VERONICA GOODRICH	0.07		
403-8	VERONICA GOODRICH	1.03		
403-9	VERONICA GOODRICH	0.56		
403-10	VERONICA GOODRICH	1.68		
403-11	VERONICA GOODRICH	0.08		
403-12	VERONICA GOODRICH	0.40		
403-13	VERONICA GOODRICH	0.08		
404-1	PORFIRIO SANTISTEVAN JR., ET UX	0.15		Warranty Deed, dtd 29 June 1968
404-2	PORFIRIO SANTISTEVAN JR., ET UX	0.15		Warranty Deed, dtd 29 June 1968
405	ALEX D. SANTISTEVAN	0.15		Warranty Deed, dtd 24 June 1968
406	VIRGINIA M MONTOYA	0.15		Warranty Deed, dtd 24 Sept 1968
407	ESTELLA A. MARTINEZ, ET AL	0.30		Warranty Deed, dtd 18 July 1968
408	MARGARITA G. MARTINEZ SANCHEZ	0.15		Warranty Deed, dtd 26 Sept 1968
409	CLARA S. KARCICH, ET AL	0.26		Warranty Deed, dtd 22 Jan 1968
410-1	LENA CARTELLI, ET AL	0.07		Warranty Deed, dtd 7 July 1970
410-2	LENA CARTELLI, ET AL	0.47		
411-1	BOARD OF COUNTY COMMISSIONERS LAS ANIMAS COUNTY, COLORADO	0.08		Warranty Deed, dtd 15 July 1970
411-2	DELETED			
411-3	DELETED			
411-4	BOARD OF COUNTY COMMISSIONERS LAS ANIMAS COUNTY, COLORADO	13.16		
412-1	SAM BRUNELLI, ET UX	0.17		Warranty Deed, dtd 5 Sept 1968
412-2	SAM BRUNELLI, ET UX	0.13		Warranty Deed, dtd 5 Sept 1968
412-3	SAM BRUNELLI, ET UX	0.22		Warranty Deed, dtd 5 Sept 1968
413-1	BOARD OF COUNTY COMMISSIONERS LAS ANIMAS COUNTY, COLORADO, ET AL	0.09		
413-2	BOARD OF COUNTY COMMISSIONERS LAS ANIMAS COUNTY, COLORADO, ET AL	0.09		
413-3	DELETED			
414	IDA L. MARTINEZ, ET VIR	0.17		Warranty Deed, dtd 7 Aug 1968
415	EDITH and ROBERT DANIEL LANGOWSKI	0.95		Warranty Deed, dtd 19 May 1969
416	DOMINIC FORNER,	0.17		Warranty Deed, dtd 5 Sept 1968
417	ALEX MONDRAGON, ET UX	0.17		Warranty Deed, dtd 24 Sept 1968
418	BARBARA RUSCETTI, AS GUARDIAN	0.26		Deed, dtd 27 May 1969
419	CHARLES LANGOWSKI	0.34		Warranty Deed, dtd 19 May 1969
420	CHAS E. LANGOWSKI	0.09		Warranty Deed, dtd 19 May 1969 Formerly known as Tract No. 413-3
421-1	JOSE A.PACHECO, ET UX	0.33		Warranty Deed, dtd 25 June 1968
421-2	JOSE A PACHECO, ET UX	0.26		Warranty Deed, dtd 25 June 1968
421-3	JOSE A PACHECO, ET UX	0.06		Warranty Deed, dtd 25 June 1968
421-4	JOSE A.PACHECO, ET UX	0.36		Warranty Deed, dtd 25 June 1968
422	MANUEL, CHARLES AND FLORA ROYBAL	0.14		Warranty Deed, dtd 20 May 1969
423	BERTHA BLASI	0.12		Warranty Deed, dtd 19 May 1969
424	LEO AND IVA FRANKLIN	0.74		Warranty Deed, dtd 19 May 1969
425	VERONICA GOODRICH	0.10		
426	GENDO AND ESTHER SEBBEN	0.14		Warranty Deed, dtd 16 July 1968
427	JOSEPHINE SKUFCA	0.34		Warranty Deed, dtd 31 Oct 1968
428-1	ANGELO BRUNELLI	0.07		Warranty Deed, dtd 7 Aug 1968
428-2	ANGELO BAUNELLI	0.08		Warranty Deed, dtd 7 Aug 1968
429	DOLLIE WILLIS	0.17		C.A. No 2357. D.T. Filed 15 June 1970
431-1	ALBERT M. CONCINI	1.30		Warranty Deed, dtd 19 May 1969
431-2	ALBERT M. CONCINI	0.22		Warranty Deed, dtd 19 May 1969
432	NICK FERROGLIO JR., ET AL	0.22		Warranty Deed, dtd 17 July 1968
433	WILLIAM J. ZANOTELLI, ET UX	0.10		Warranty Deed, dtd 16 July 1968
434	JIMMIE E. BONATO, ET UX	0.22		Warranty Deed, dtd 25 June 1968
435	DOMINICK FERRARO, ET AL	0.29		Warranty Deed, dtd 4 June 1969
436	ANTONIO E. SANTISTEVAN, ET UX	0.29		Warranty Deed, dtd 25 June 1968
437	JOE ARTHUR SANTISTEVAN, ET UX	0.26		Warranty Deed, dtd 26 June 1968
438	ANNA LONG, ET AL	0.10		Warranty Deed, dtd 26 Sept 1968
439	HARRY L. BEIRNE, ADMINISTRATOR OF THE ESTATE OF DOMENICA CAFFARO	0.14		Deed, dtd 23 June 1969
441	VICTOR MACCHIETTO, ET UX	0.14		Warranty Deed, dtd 12 Aug 1968
442	FRANK CONCINI, ET AL	0.14		Warranty Deed, dtd 25 Sept 1968
443-1	ANGELO BRUNELLI	0.36		Warranty Deed, dtd 15 July 1968
443-2	ANGELO BRUNELLI	0.14		Warranty Deed, dtd 15 July 1968
444	T.C. ANTISTA	0.14		Warranty Deed, dtd 9 July 1970
445	SOCIETA FRATELLI UNITI AND THE SILVIO PELLICO SOCIETY	0.31		Warranty Deed, dtd 16 Dec 1968
446	TONY CAMBRUZZI, ET AL	0.16		Warranty Deed, dtd 19 May 1969
447	VIRGINIA CORRA	0.20		Warranty Deed, dtd 21 May 1970
448	GUISUFIA LIRA	0.43		Warranty Deed, dtd 8 July 1970
449	E.H. BOWLDEN	0.22		Warranty Deed, dtd 6 Aug 1968
451	ANGELO VECELLIO, ET UX	0.22		Warranty Deed, dtd 16 July 1968
452	ERNEST BELLEGANTE	0.14		Warranty Deed, dtd 25 Sept 1968
453	FRANK SHABLO	0.16		Warranty Deed, dtd 19 Dec 1969
454	DOMINICK FERRERO	0.41		Warranty Deed, dtd 26 Jul 1968
455	VICTOR DONA	0.31		Warranty Deed, dtd 26 June 1968
456	ALBERT MACCHIETTO, ET UX	0.28		Warranty Deed, dtd 15 July 1968

TRACT NO.	LAND OWNER	ACREAGE FEE	EASM'T	REMARKS
457	PAUL MILANESE, EXECUTOR OF THE ESTATE OF ATTILIO MONTIBELLER	0.28		Warranty Deed, dtd 26 Sept 1968
458	MARIA CALLOVINI	0.14		Warranty Deed, dtd 24 June 1968
459	ERNEST FALAGRADY, ET AL	0.14		Warranty Deed, dtd 25 June 1968
461	MARY THOMPSON	0.14		Warranty Deed, dtd 18 July 1968
462	O.F. ADAMS, CONSERVATOR FOR ERNESTO TURRA	0.14		Deed, dtd 6 Aug 1968
463	MIKE BUTERO	0.83		Warranty Deed, dtd 25 June 1968
464	UNKNOWN	4.54		

LEGEND
~ 6,230'~ Top of Conservation Pool
~ 6,260'~ Top of Flood Control Pool
~ 6,263'~ Acquisition Guide Line

SEGMENT MAP INDEX
ONE INCH EQUALS APPROXIMATELY 3,520'

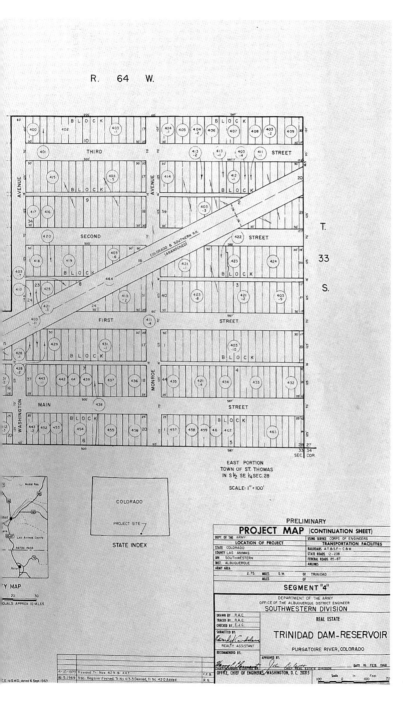

Eastern portion
of St. Thomas.

TRACT REGISTER

TRACT NO.	LAND OWNER	ACREAGE FEE	EASMT	REMARKS
500-1	MARY A. DAUGHERTY, ET AL	0.82		Warranty Deed, dated
500-2	MARY A. DAUGHERTY, ET AL	0.09		Warranty Deed, dated
500-3	DELETED	—		
501-1	VERONICA GOODRICH	0.22		Warranty Deed, dated
501-2	VERONICA GOODRICH	0.30		Warranty Deed, dated
501-3	VERONICA GOODRICH	0.07		Warranty Deed, dated
501-4	VERONICA GOODRICH	0.15		Warranty Deed, dated
501-5	VERONICA GOODRICH	0.57		Warranty Deed, dated
501-6	VERONICA GOODRICH	0.06		Warranty Deed, dated
501-7	VERONICA GOODRICH	1.38		Warranty Deed, dated
501-8	VERONICA GOODRICH	0.09		Warranty Deed, dated
501-9	VERONICA GOODRICH	1.12		Warranty Deed, dated
501-10	VERONICA GOODRICH	0.18		Warranty Deed, dated
501-11	VERONICA GOODRICH	1.46		Warranty Deed, dated
501-12	VERONICA GOODRICH	0.66		Warranty Deed, dated
501-13	VERONICA GOODRICH	0.65		Warranty Deed, dated
501-14	VERONICA GOODRICH	0.40		Warranty Deed, dated
501-15	VERONICA GOODRICH	0.14		Warranty Deed, dated
501-16	VERONICA GOODRICH	0.21		Warranty Deed, dated
501-17	VERONICA GOODRICH	0.06		Warranty Deed, dated
502	THOMAS FERRARO	0.25		Warranty Deed, dated 18 Dec. 1969
503	CHARLES LONG	0.07		Warranty Deed, dated 19 May 1969
504-1	JOSE A. PACHECO	0.07		Warranty Deed, dated 25 June 1968
504-2	JOSE A. PACHECO	0.09		Warranty Deed, dated 25 June 1968
505	PATRICK SANDOVAL, ET AL	0.07		C.A. No. 2357 D/T Filed 15 June 1970
506	PETE ARCHULETTA	0.67		Warranty Deed, dated 24 June 1968
507	DOLLIE WILLIS	0.09		C.A. No. 2357 D/T Filed 15 June 1970
508	TOM FERRERO, ET UX	1.35		Warranty Deed, dated
508-2	TOM FERRERO, ET UX	0.54 / 0.50		Warranty Deed, dated 18 Dec. 1969
510	BOARD OF COUNTY COMMISSIONERS LAS ANIMAS COUNTY COLO.	0.08		
511	JOSEPHINE THOMPSON, ET AL	0.09		C.A. No. 2357 D/T Filed 15 June 1970
512	ALFREDO E. & ISABELLO ARGUELLO	0.09		Warranty Deed, dated 21 May 1969
513	BILL G. CORDOVA, ET UX	0.17		C.A. No. 2357 D/T Filed 15 June 1970
514	FLOYD CORDOVA, ET AL	0.26		Warranty Deed, dated 18 Dec. 1969
515	JOSEPH MARTIN, ET AL	0.09		Warranty Deed, dated
516	JUAN R. & CELIA B. LOVATO	0.20		Warranty Deed, dated 19 May 1969
517	ASSED JOSEPH	0.17		C.A. No. 2357 D/T Filed 15 June 1970
518	LAS ANIMAS COUNTY	0.09		Warranty Deed, dated 28 August 1970
519	DELETED	—		
520	WILLIAM MUSSELWHITE	0.08		
521	BISHOP, ROMAN CATHOLIC CHURCH	0.60		Warranty Deed, dated 4 March 1970
522	DAVID SKUFCA	0.17		Warranty Deed, dated 31 Oct. 1968
523	MRS. SYLVESTER JOSEPHINE SKUFCA	0.60		Warranty Deed, dated 19 May 1969
524	FIDEL ALEX MARTINEZ, ET UX	0.29		Warranty Deed, dated 15 July 1968
525	SAM ARTHUR BRUNELLI, ET AL	1.30		Warranty Deed, dated 16 Aug 1968
526	WESTON O. THOMAS, ET UX	0.34		Warranty Deed, dated 24 June 1968
527	JOHN BERGANT, ET UX	0.17		Warranty Deed, dated 16 July 1968
528	MIKE MARTORANO, ET UX	0.17		Warranty Deed, dated 24 June 1968
529	JOHN J. JOHNSON, ET UX	0.26		Warranty Deed, dated 7 July 1970
529-2	GARFIELD JOHNSON	0.09		Warranty Deed, dated
531	JOSEFITA L. SANCHEZ	0.12		Warranty Deed, dated 25 Sept 1968
532	APOLONIO LOPEZ, ET AL	0.43		Warranty Deed, dated 25 Sept 1968
533-1	BOARD OF COUNTY COMMISSIONERS LAS ANIMAS COUNTY COLO.	10.42		Warranty Deed, dated
533-2	BOARD OF COUNTY COMMISSIONERS LAS ANIMAS COUNTY COLO.	0.26		Warranty Deed, dated 28 August 1970
533-3	BOARD OF COUNTY COMMISSIONERS LAS ANIMAS COUNTY COLO.	0.17		Warranty Deed, dated 28 August 1970
533-4	BOARD OF COUNTY COMMISSIONERS LAS ANIMAS COUNTY COLO.	0.57		Warranty Deed, dated 28 August 1970
533-5	BOARD OF COUNTY COMMISSIONERS LAS ANIMAS COUNTY COLO.	0.43		Warranty Deed, dated
534	GABRIEL VIGIL	0.32		Warranty Deed, dated 21 May 1969
535	EVA MARTINEZ	0.17		Warranty Deed, dated 30 June 1969
536	GEORGE A. NEWSAM JR, ET AL	0.17		Warranty Deed, dated
537	E. W. RITCHIE, ET AL	0.26		Warranty Deed, dated 20 June 1969
538	NESTOR MARTINEZ, ET UX	0.34		Warranty Deed, dated 21 May 1969
539	MANUEL CHARLES AND FLORA ROYBAL	0.17		Warranty Deed, dated 20 May 1969
540-1	MARK D. ARGO, ET AL	0.01		
540-2	MARK D. ARGO, ET AL	0.03		

TRACT REGISTER

TRACT NO.	LAND OWNER	ACREAGE FEE	EASMT	REMARKS
541-1	CLARA S. KARCICH	0.39		Warranty Deed, dated 22 JAN. 1969
541-2	CLARA S. KARCICH	0.34		Warranty Deed, dated 22 JAN. 1969
541-3	CLARA S. KARCICH	0.26		Warranty Deed, dated 22 JAN. 1969
542	CLARA S. KARCICH	0.17		Warranty Deed, dated 22 JAN. 1969
543	FRANK J. MARTINI, ET AL	0.09		Warranty Deed, dated 22 JAN. 1969
544	JOE T. MARTINEZ, ET UX	0.14		Warranty Deed, dated 6 Aug. 1968
545	DAVID M. MENAPACE, ET AL	0.29		Warranty Deed, dated 25 June 1968
546	ROY BACA, ET UX	0.14		Warranty Deed, dated 7 Aug 1968
547	SALVADOR MARTORANO, ET UX	0.18		Warranty Deed, dated 17 July 1968
548	JOSEPH MARTORANO, ET AL	0.11		Warranty Deed, dated 18 July 1968
549	CARMEL A. GARLUTZO, EXECUTOR OF THE ESTATE OF JOE LUCCIA	0.14		Warranty Deed, dated 16 June 1969
551	TONY CAMBRUZZI, ET AL	0.21		Warranty Deed, dated 19 May 1969
552	DELETE	—		
553	MAXINE VIGIL	0.14		Warranty Deed, dated 24 Sept 1968
554	CARMEL A. GARLUTZO, EXECUTOR OF THE ESTATE OF JOE LUCCIA	0.14		Warranty Deed, dated 16 June 1969
555	PAUL BUTERI	0.22		Warranty Deed, dated 18 Dec. 1969
556	JAMES BUCCOLA	0.14		Warranty Deed, dated 19 May 1969
557	CARMEL A. GARLUTZO, EXECUTOR OF THE ESTATE OF JOE LUCCIA	0.07		Warranty Deed, dated 16 June 1969
558	CARMEL A. GARLUTZO, EXECUTOR OF THE ESTATE OF JOE LUCCIA	0.36		Warranty Deed, dated 16 June 1969
559	UNKNOWN	0.88		
501-18	VERONICA GOODRICH	0.09		Warranty Deed, dated

PROJECT SITE

COLORADO
NEW MEXICO

VICINITY MAP

SCALE IN MILES ONE INCH EQUALS APPROXIMATELY 10 MILES

COLORADO

PROJECT SITE

STATE INDEX

SEGMENT MAP INDEX
ONE INCH EQUALS APPROXIMATELY 3520'

LEGEND

~ 6,230' ~ Top of Conservation Pool
~ 6,26 ' ~ Top of Flood Control Pool
~ 6,26 3' ~ Acquisition Guide Line

184

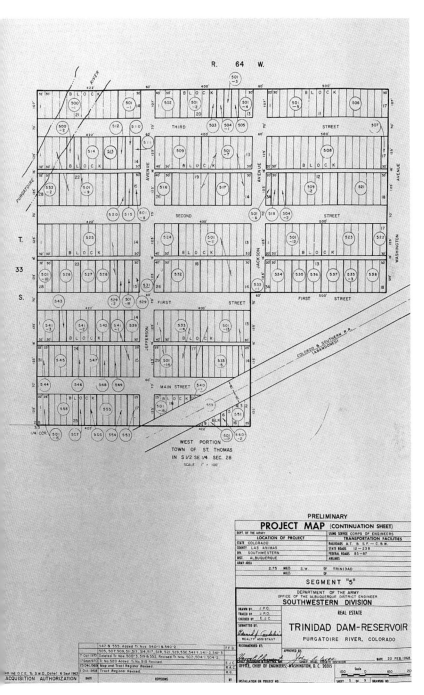

Western portion of St. Thomas.

185

TRACT REGISTER

TRACT NO.	LAND OWNER	ACREAGE FEE	EASM'T	REMARKS
601-1	DELETED	—		
601-2	DELETED	—		
601-3	C.F.&I. STEEL CORPORATION	0.16		
601-4	C.F.&I. STEEL CORPORATION	0.16		
602	JASPER BUTERO, ET UX	0.14		Warranty Deed, dtd 15 May 1969
603	LEE LUCERO, ET UX	0.12		Warranty Deed, dtd 24 Sept. 1968
604	ALDO SEBBEN, ET UX	0.10		Warranty Deed, dtd 26 Sept. 1968
605	ADOLPH SEBBEN, ET UX	0.23		Warranty Deed, dtd 5 Sept. 1968
606	LUCY COSZALTER	0.06		Warranty Deed, dtd 15 July 1968
607	ALFRED LAIMINGER, ET UX	0.11		Warranty Deed, dtd 24 Sept 1968
608-1	SCHOOL DISTRICT NO. 1	0.52		Special Warranty Deed, dtd 7 Aug 1968
608-2	SCHOOL DISTRICT NO. 1	0.40		Special Warranty Deed, dtd 7 Aug 1968
608-3	SCHOOL DISTRICT NO. 1	0.17		Special Warranty Deed, dtd 7 Aug 1968
608-4	SCHOOL DISTRICT NO. 1	0.34		Special Warranty Deed, dtd 7 Aug 1968
608-5	SCHOOL DISTRICT NO. 1	0.50		Special Warranty Deed, dtd 7 Aug 1968
609	JOE INCITTI, ET UX	0.17		Warranty Deed, dtd 6 Aug 1968
611	VIRGINIA AND GINO LIRA	0.11		Warranty Deed, dtd 15 July 1968
612	ROSE SEBBEN	0.11		Warranty Deed, dtd 23 June 1969
613	ANGELO AND LAURA DeANGELIS	0.17		Warranty Deed, dtd 7 Aug 1968
614-1	G. PASSERO, ET AL	0.11		Warranty Deed, dtd 26 June 1968
614-2	G. PASSERO, ET AL	0.11		Warranty Deed, dtd 26 June 1968
615	FRANK MACHOVE, ET UX	0.11		Warranty Deed, dtd 7 Aug 1968
616	VITA ZOMPARELLI	0.25		Warranty Deed, dtd 15 Aug 1969
617	BRUNO FALDUTO	0.75		Warranty Deed, dtd 23 June 1969
618	LOUIS N. BONATO, ET AL	0.29		Warranty Deed, dtd 7 Aug 1968
619-1	AUGUST ZAMBORELLI, ET UX	0.17		Warranty Deed, dtd 7 Aug 1968
619-2	AUGUST ZAMBORELLI, ET UX	0.11		Warranty Deed, dtd 7 Aug 1968
621	ROCCO DeANGELIS, ET UX	0.13		Warranty Deed, dtd 7 Aug 1968
622	JAMES BUCCOLA	0.34		Warranty Deed, dtd 19 May 1969
623	DELETED	—		
624	VITA ZAMPARELLI	0.34		Warranty Deed, dtd 15 Aug 1969
625	JOHN DONACHY, ET UX	0.11		Warranty Deed, dtd 24 Sept. 1969
626	JOSEPH SEBBEN, ET UX	0.11		Warranty Deed, dtd 24 Sept 1968
627	DAN ARCHULETA, ET UX	0.11		Warranty Deed, dtd 31 Oct 1968
628	JOHN F. COSTA, ADMINISTRATOR	0.11		Administrator's Deed, dtd 19 May 1969
629	MARY IDA AND ROSE SEBBEN	0.11		Warranty Deed, dtd 31 Oct 1968
631	SAM TERRY, ET UX	0.23		Warranty Deed, dtd 31 Oct 1968
632	ANGELO FADRO, ET UX	0.23		Warranty Deed, dtd 24 Sept 1968
633	EMMA T. WATSON	0.11		Warranty Deed, dtd 24 Sept 1968
634	TONY D. CORDOVA	0.11		Warranty Deed, dtd 1 Aug 1968
635	ALBERT VECELLIO, ET UX	0.11		Warranty Deed, dtd 24 Sept 1968
636-1	JOHN ANTISTA	0.23		Warranty Deed, dtd 31 Oct 1968
636-2	JOHN ANTISTA	0.23		Warranty Deed, dtd 31 Oct 1968
637	CHARLES B. MARTORANO	0.11		Warranty Deed, dtd 19 May 1969
638	SENTINO R. COSZALTER, ET UX	0.23		Warranty Deed, dtd 21 May 1969
639	JOE SLANOVICH, ET UX	0.11		Warranty Deed, dtd 7 Aug 1968
641-1	IRENE CERAME, ET VIR	0.11		Warranty Deed, dtd 7 Aug 1968
641-2	IRENE CERAME, ET VIR	0.11		Warranty Deed, dtd 7 Aug 1968
642	JOHN VECELLIO	0.11		Warranty Deed, dtd 24 Sept. 1968
643	EZEQUIEL LUCERO, ET AL	0.23		Warranty Deed, dtd 7 Aug 1968
644	CLARA SANCHEZ, ET AL	0.11		Warranty Deed, dtd 25 June 1969
645	LOUIS REGUSA, ET UX	0.23		Warranty Deed, dtd 23 June 1969
646	NICK FURIA	0.11		Warranty Deed, dtd 19 May 1969
647	EZEQUIEL SANCHEZ, ET UX	0.23		Warranty Deed, dtd 11 Aug 1969
648	FRANK MARTINEZ	0.11		Warranty Deed, dtd 20 May 1969
649	FURU REALTY AND INVESTMENT COMPANY	0.11		Warranty Deed, dtd 22 May 1969
651-1	JOE DeANGELIS, ET AL	0.23		Warranty Deed, dtd 24 June 1969
651-2	JOE DeANGELIS, ET AL	0.23		Warranty Deed, dtd 24 June 1969
652	CHURCH OF JESUS CHRIST A CORPORATION OF MONONGAHELA, PENN.	0.11		Warranty Deed, dtd 16 June 1969
653	LENA FERRI	0.18		Warranty Deed, dtd 24 June 1969
654	ALFRED SANTISTEVAN, ET UX	0.11		Warranty Deed, dtd 19 May 1969
655	ANGELO ZANCANERO, ET UX	0.11		Warranty Deed, dtd 24 Sept 1968
656	ANGELO ZANCANERO, ET UX	0.11		Warranty Deed, dtd 26 Sept 1968
657	NATHAN LOUIS LIRA	0.23		Warranty Deed, dtd 24 Sept 1968
658	JOHN P. COSZALTER	0.11		Warranty Deed, dtd 19 May 1969
659	JOHN COSSALTER, ET UX	0.11		Warranty Deed, dtd 11 Aug 1969
661	ERCIE VIGIL	0.11		Warranty Deed, dtd 31 Oct 1969
662	MARY ANN JURNEKE SKINNER	0.11		Warranty Deed, dtd 9 Sept 1968
663	RICARDO AND PETE S. COSSALTER	0.11		Warranty Deed, dtd 19 May 1969
664	BOARD OF COUNTY COMMISSIONERS LAS ANIMAS COUNTY	6.97		
665	LENA FERRI, ET AL	0.05		Warranty Deed, dtd 24 June 1969

SEGMENT MAP INDEX
ONE INCH EQUALS APPROXIMATELY 3,520

VICINITY MAP
SCALE IN MILES ONE INCH EQUALS APPROX 10 MILES

COLORADO

PROJECT SITE

STATE INDEX

LEGEND
—6,230— Top of Conservation
—6,260— Top of Flood Control
—6,263— Acquisition Guide L

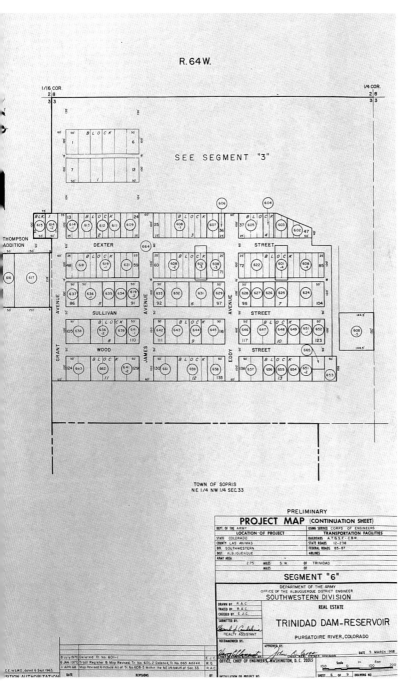

Main Sopris.

187

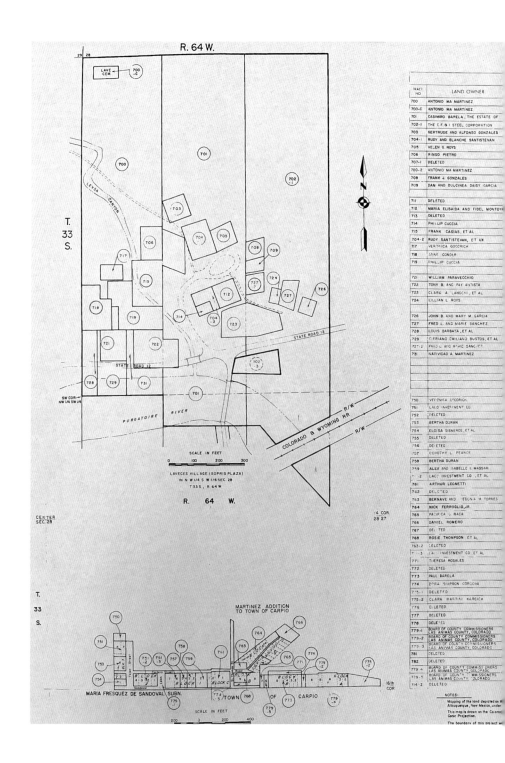

TRACT NO.	LAND OWNER
700	ANTONIO MA MARTINEZ
700-C	ANTONIO MA MARTINEZ
701	CASIMIRO BARELA, THE ESTATE OF
702-1	THE C.F. & I STEEL CORPORATION
703	GERTRUDE AND ALFONSO GONZALES
704-1	RUDY AND BLANCHE SANTISTEVAN
705	HELEN G. ROYS
706	RINGO PIETRO
707-1	DELETED
700-2	ANTONIO MA MARTINEZ
708	FRANK J. GONZALES
709	DAN AND DULCINEA DAISY GARCIA
711	DELETED
712	MARIA ELISAIDA AND FIDEL MONTOYA
713	DELETED
714	PHILLIP CUCCIA
715	FRANK CASIAS, ET AL
704-2	RUDY SANTISTEVAN, ET UX
717	VERONICA GOODRICH
718	ANNE CONDER
719	PHILLIP CUCCIA
721	WILLIAM PARAVECCHIO
722	TONY B. AND FAY ANTISTA
723	CLARA A. LANGONI, ET AL
724	LILLIAN L. ROYS
726	JOHN B. AND MARY M. GARCIA
727	FRED L. AND MARIE SANCHEZ
728	LOUIS BARBATA, ET AL
729	CIPRIANO EMILIANO BUSTOS, ET AL
727-2	FRED L. AND MARIE SANCHEZ
731	NATIVIDAD A. MARTINEZ
750	VERONICA GOODRICH
751	LACC INVESTMENT CO.
752	DELETED
753	BERTHA DURAN
754	ELOISA SISNEROS, ET AL
755	DELETED
756	DELETED
757	DOROTHY L. PEARCE
758	BERTHA DURAN
759	ALEX AND ISABELLE I. MASSARI
759-2	LACC INVESTMENT CO., ET AL
761	ARTHUR LEONETTI
762	DELETED
763	BERNAVE AND EDONIA M. TORRES
764	NICK FERROGLIO, JR.
765	PACIFICA G. BACA
766	DANIEL ROMERO
767	DELETED
768	ROSIE THOMPSON ET AL
763-2	DELETED
769-3	LACC INVESTMENT CO. ET AL
771	THERESA ROSALES
772	DELETED
773	PAUL BARELA
774	DORA SIMPSON CORDOVA
775-1	DELETED
775-2	CLARA MARTINI KARCICH
776	DELETED
777	DELETED
778	DELETED
779-1	BOARD OF COUNTY COMMISSIONERS LAS ANIMAS COUNTY, COLORADO
779-2	BOARD OF COUNTY COMMISSIONERS LAS ANIMAS COUNTY, COLORADO
779-3	BOARD OF COUNTY COMMISSIONERS LAS ANIMAS COUNTY, COLORADO
781	DELETED
782	DELETED
779-4	BOARD OF COUNTY COMMISSIONERS LAS ANIMAS COUNTY, COLORADO
779-5	BOARD OF COUNTY COMMISSIONERS LAS ANIMAS COUNTY, COLORADO
714-2	DELETED

NOTES:
Mapping of the land depicted on this plat was done in Albuquerque, New Mexico, under...
This map is drawn on the Colorado Conic Projection.
The boundary of this project was...

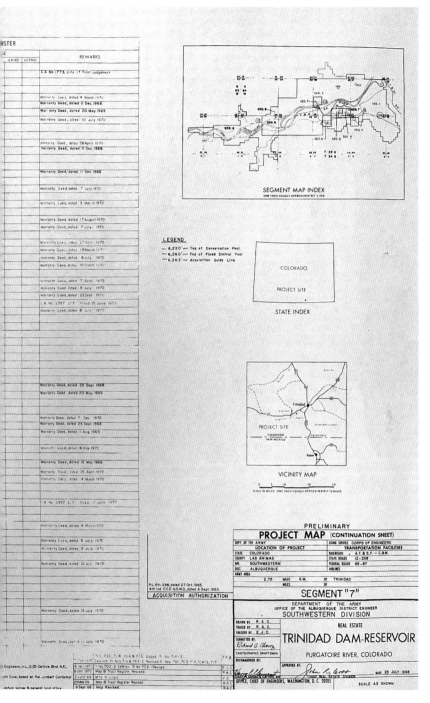

Sopris Plaza and town of Carpio with Martinez Addition and Maria Fresquez de Sandoval Subdivision.

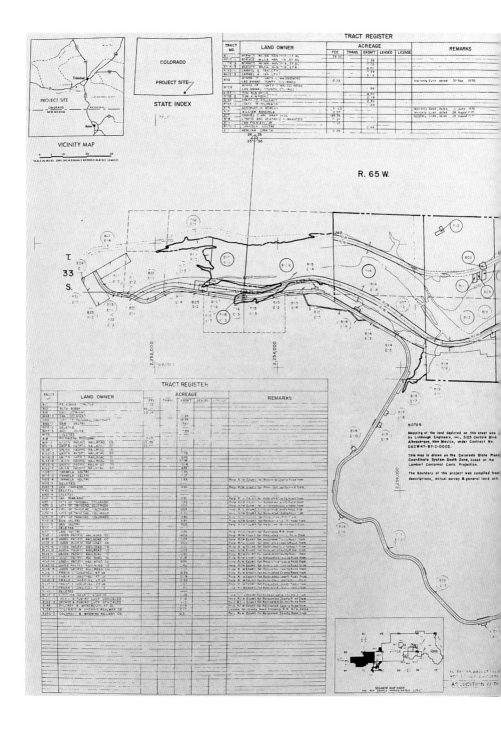

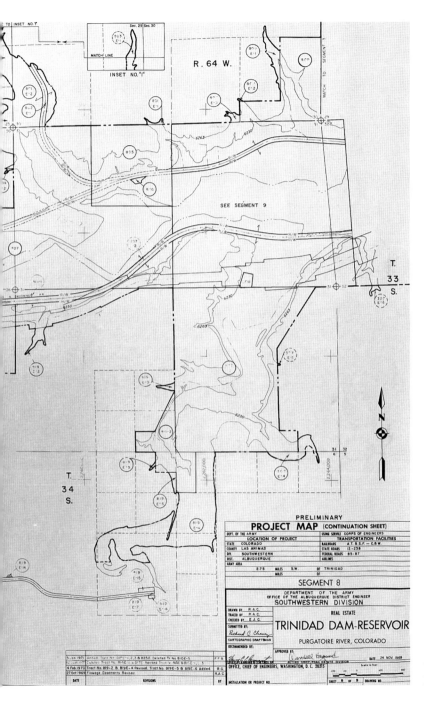

Westernmost landowners.

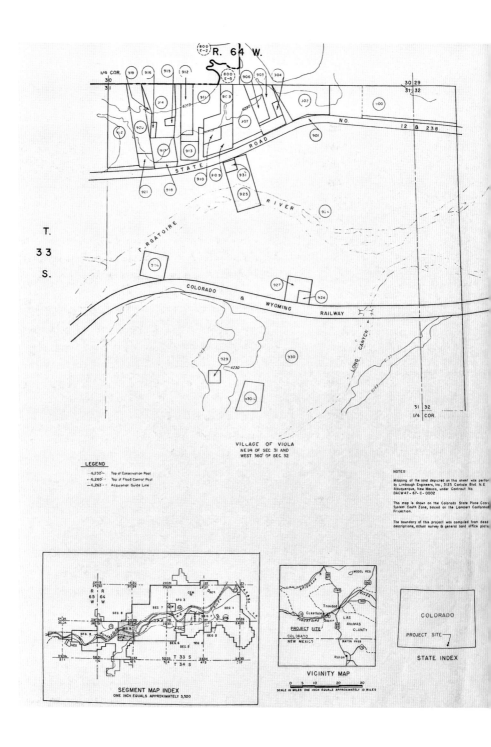

TRACT REGISTER

TRACT NO.	LAND OWNER	ACREAGE						REMARKS
		FEE	TRANS	LEASED	EASM'T	LICENSE	PERMIT	
900	JOHN C. TAPIA	6.49						
901	BOARD OF COUNTY COMMISSIONERS LAS ANIMAS COUNTY, COLORADO	4.25						
902	GEORGE J ROMERO	2.31						
903	ROSITA M ARGUELLO	0.87						Warranty Deed, dated 1 Dec 1970
904	FURU REALTY & INVESTMENT CO.	0.14						Warranty Deed, dated 27 August 1970
906	GABRIEL ARGUELLO	0.49						Warranty Deed, dated 1 Dec 1970
907	TRINIDAD INDUSTRIAL BANK	2.12						
908	WILLIAM GONZALES, ET AL	1.09						Warranty Deed, dated 1 Dec 1970
909	FRANK AND AMALIA SALVADOR	0.80						Warranty Deed, dated 31 August 1970
910	ROSE MARY ORTEGA	0.34						Warranty Deed, dated 26 August 1970
911	RUDY SANTISTEVAN, ET AL	1.82						Warranty Deed, dated 1 Dec 1970
912	RALPH GARCIA	0.94						Warranty Deed, dated 26 August 1970
913	MIKE NICCOLI, ET AL	0.52						Warranty Deed, dated 3 Oct 1970
914	SAM BACA SR , ET UX	1.96						Warranty Deed, dated 24 August 1970
915	ANNABELLE ROYBAL, ET AL	0.12						Warranty Deed, dated 26 August 1970
916	SAM BACA, JR , ET UX	0.14						Warranty Deed, dated 12 Dec 1970
917	BEN GARCIA, ET AL	0.92						Warranty Deed, dated 1 Dec 1970
918	ISAAC DURAN	0.20						Warranty Deed, dated 25 August 1970
919	UNKNOWN	0.25						
920	DELFINO & SEDEALIA SANTISTEVAN	1.64						Warranty Deed dated 2 Dec 1970
921	TIM GONZALEZ	0.32						Warranty Deed, dated 25 August 1970
922	JOE E. & FANNIE G MONTOYA	1.26						Warranty Deed, dated 31 August 1970
923	COLORADO & WYOMING RAILWAY	6.61						
924	ANNIE KOKOTOVICK	83.61						
925	MARY KUCHAR	1.76						Warranty Deed, dated 3 Dec 1970
926	FLORENCE MACHINERY AND SUPPLY COMPANY	0.92						
927	LENA MONTOYA	0.69						Warranty Deed, dated 1 Dec 1970
928	MARIA PERFECTA ROYBAL	0.23						
929	FRATERNIDAD PIADOSA DE NUESTRO SENOR SAN JOSE	0.23						
930	ROY BACA	55.61						Warranty Deed, dated 24 August 1970
930-C	ROY BACA	0.97						I.A. No. 1773 DrT Filed
931	MARY KUCHAR, ET AL	0.20						Warranty Deed, dated 1 Dec 1970

PRELIMINARY

PROJECT MAP (CONTINUATION SHEET)

DEPT. OF THE ARMY		USING SERVICE CORPS OF ENGINEERS
LOCATION OF PROJECT		TRANSPORTATION FACILITIES
STATE	COLORADO	RAILROADS A.T. & S.F. - C.& W.
COUNTY	LAS ANIMAS	STATE ROADS 12 - 236
DIV.	SOUTHWESTERN	FEDERAL ROADS 85 - 87
DIST.	ALBUQUERQUE	AIRLINES
ARMY AREA		

2.75 MILES S. W. OF TRINIDAD
MILES OF

SEGMENT 9

DEPARTMENT OF THE ARMY
OFFICE OF THE ALBUQUERQUE DISTRICT ENGINEER
SOUTHWESTERN DIVISION

DRAWN BY	R.G.	REAL ESTATE
TRACED BY	R.G.	
CHECKED BY	E.J.C.	

TRINIDAD DAM-RESERVOIR

PURGATOIRE RIVER, COLORADO

DATE 24 NOV 1969
ACTING CHIEF, REAL ESTATE DIVISION
OFFICE, CHIEF OF ENGINEERS, WASHINGTON, D. C. 20315

SCALE IN FEET
200 0 200 400
SHEET 9 OF 9 DRAWING NO

8 Sept 1973 Added Tr. 931 and Revised Tr 925
23 July 1970 Added Contours & Project Boundary
2 June 1970, Tr Nos. 924 & 925 Revised

1965
dated 6 Sept 1963.
AUTHORIZATION DATE REVISIONS

Viola and
Madrid Plaza.

Appendix C

STATE MINING INSPECTOR'S REPORT

SOPRIS MINE NO. 2 EXPLOSION ON MARCH 24, 1922

The following four pages, from the *Tenth Annual Report of the State Inspector of Coal Mines 1922*, contain the report of W.M. Laurie, deputy state inspector of coal mines, on the explosion at Sopris Mine No. 2 on March 24, 1922

REPORT ON SOPRIS NO. 2 MINE EXPLOSION

April 28, 1922.

Mr. James Dalrymple,
State Inspector of Coal Mines,
Capitol Building,
Denver, Colo.

Dear Sir:

The following is my report concerning the explosion at Sopris No. 2 mine, which occurred on the afternoon of March 24th, 1922.

The mine is situated four miles west of Trinidad, Las Animas county, Colorado, on the Colorado & Southern Railroad, and is operated by the Colorado Fuel & Iron Co. The mine is opened by two parallel slopes, course East of South, 700 feet long. The slope dips 15%, the manway 20%, from this point the mine is practically level.

The mine is ventilated by a steam exhaust, reversible fan, 6x12 feet, double port of entry, steel type, made by the Colorado Fuel & Iron Company and was installed 50 feet, at right angles, from air-shaft. The volume of air entering the mine varied from 80,000 to 90,000 cubic feet per minute under three-inch water gauge and was conducted into the different districts by the split system, there being six splits.

The air upon entering the mine is pre-heated by radiators. Steam is then thrown into it for the purpose of furnishing all the moisture it will carry. The relative humidity readings taken by Deputy State Coal Mine Inspector, semi-annually, during summer and winter months varies but very little, if any, and run from 90 to 100. In addition to this, haulage roads were sprinkled frequently, part by hose from pipe line and part by water car.

Haulage system was by rope, electric motors, and mules. The voltage for electric motors was 550 D.C., and for electric machines and pumps, 440 A.C. Haulage motors and electric pumps were on the intake air. Electric head lamps were used exclusively, except mine officials.

Superintendent, mine foreman, assistant mine foreman, fire bosses, and shot firers use safety lamps for detection of explosive gas. All shots were fired at night by electric hand batteries, only permissible powder being used.

The mining of coal was done by hand on the east side of mine. Main slopes and west side of mine by electric machines.

At 4 o'clock in the afternoon of March 24th, 1922, I was notified by telephone through the office of the Colorado Fuel & Iron Co. that Sopris Mine No. 2 had exploded and that from 75 to 80 men were entombed, but by checking out the men it was found that all men were out but 17, who lost their lives. I immediately went to the mine and upon my arrival there found that the fan was still intact and in operation. The explosion doors to fan were blown out, thus disconnecting the fan from the mine until temporary repairs were made, when the ventilation was partly restored in the mine.

On entering the mine I found the Superintendent, Mine Foreman, Fire Bosses, and several others, building temporary stoppings along the main haulage road restoring the ventilation as rapidly as possible. The rebuilding of temporary stoppings was continued until 3:30 a. m. the morning of the 25th and progressed to within 500 feet of slope faces, when the shift which had continuously worked from the time of the explosion was withdrawn until that district could be cleared of gases. This shift was relieved by another shift, who after several hours found the bodies of the slope men.

The east side of the mine was explored by Mr. McAllister, C. F. & I. Mine Inspector, fire bosses, two others and myself, and we found that the point of ignition was not in the east side of the mine. The slopes and west side of the mine were explored by D. M. Harrington, U. S. Bureau of Mines, Robert McAllister, Company Inspector, State Inspector of Coal Mines, three Deputy Inspectors, and mine officials, who found that all permanent stoppings had been destroyed between the main intake and return airway, from the foot of 700-foot slope to face of main slopes, except three, which were left intact. All over-casts, under-casts, and doors were destroyed except one over-cast, which had been lately constructed on new airway, east side of mine.

There were four electric Sullivan latest type C. E. 7, gas proof machines carrying U. S. Bureau of Mines permissible plates. Three of them were in the 7th and 8th west entries. These machines ordinarily started cutting about 3:00 p. m. and quit about 11:00 p. m. Machine No. 1 was found in 8th west back entry still on its truck. Machine No. 2 was found in room No. 3 off room No. 9, 14 cut-off, set up and ready to start. Machine No. 3 was found in room No. 49, 7th west entry. This machine apparently was in operation when the explosion occurred, but there were no signs of heat or violence within three or four hundred feet of this machine. The power apparently had been cut off by the men before leaving. Their bodies were found 800 feet from the machine. Machine No. 4 was employed in the main slopes, cutting here was done during the day. The machine was found on main slope, apparently it had been brought from the right back slope, as the feed cable was still there.

There are three places in the mine, either of which might have been the initial point. They are as follows: The 8th west right back entry, room No. 3 off room No. 9, 14 cut-off, and right hand back slope. All of these places generate explosive gas, especially the latter, and all of them are equally dependent on doors for ventilation. The leaving open of a door or doors at either place for 20 or 30 minutes would allow an accumulation of explosive gas. In the right back slope it would be greater than at either of the other two.

At the inquest it was brought out that there was no regular fire boss examining the places on the afternoon shift, as the regular night fire boss did not come on shift until 4:00 o'clock, which was two hours after the machine men had entered. Therefore, some places may have been cleaned up several hours before machine men entered to cut them, and in all probabilities a considerable body of gas was generated in the meantime.

The scouring on sides of main slope 7th west entry into room No. 1 and the condition of cars on main slope at 5th east parting, where parts of cars had been blown outward and inward, also coke deposits on inside and outside of timbers, indicate that double action had taken place. This evidence does not exist in other parts of the mine, where there was considerable room for expansion. Here there was very little sign of violence, but intense heat, timbers being charred deeply on all sides, with considerable deposits of coke all over them. The scouring on main slope and 7 west entry into room No. 1 indicate that last force came out of the 7th west entry and down main slope, destroying to some extent the scouring made by the previous force traveling in the opposite direction.

In conclusion, the catastrophe was an explosion of gas and dust, caused by an accumulation of gas through a door or doors being left open, and ignited by an electric arc, and that in all probability the right back slope was the initial point.

Respectfully submitted,

W. M. LAURIE,
Deputy State Inspector of Coal Mines.
District No. 1.

Explosion at the Sopris mine in which 17 lives were lost:

March 24—PETE ADAMO, American, machine helper, age 33 years, married, two children.

FRANCESCO AMETEIS, Italian, pick miner, age 23 years, single.

ANTONIO BERTETTO, Italian, pick miner, age 22 years, single.

GUISEPPE BONATO, American, pick miner, age 64 years, married, two children.

MIGUEL CAUDILLO, Mexican, machine loader, age 28 years, married, no children.

MAX COVI, Austrian, machine runner, age 44 years, married, four children.

PETE DELDOSSO, American, runner and machine miner, age 24 years, married, one child.

FELIX MAGLIA, Italian, pick miner, age 24 years, single.

JOE MARLO, American, runner and machine miner, age 33 years, married, one child.

PETE MUSIAL, Polish, pick miner, age 36 years, married, one child and three step-children.

RUDOLPH PEASHKA, American, pick miner, age 36 years, married, four children.

CHARLES ROMERO, American, machine runner, age 45 years, married, seven children.

ROBERT E. ROMERO, American, machine helper, age 18 years, single.

PETE L. SAVIO, American, runner and machine miner, age 25 years, married, one child.

ODILAN SERRANO, Mexican, machine miner, age 47 years, widower, two children.

FRANK VALENCHICH, Slav, machine runner, age 32 years, married, no children.

MATT VALENCHICH, Slav, machine runner, age 28 years, married, two children.

FRANK EVANS'S 1972 CONGRESSIONAL STATEMENT

The following four pages contain the statement by Frank Evans to the House Committee on Public Works, June 15, 1972.

STATEMENT BY THE HONORABLE FRANK E. EVANS OF COLORADO
BEFORE THE HOUSE COMMITTEE ON PUBLIC WORKS,
SUBCOMMITTEE ON ROADS

June 15, 1972

Mr. Chairman, thank you for granting me the privilege of testifying on possible amendments to the Relocation Assistance Act of 1970.

My purpose here today is to urge the Committee to consider extending the relocation benefits of Public Law 91-646 to certain categories of people who have been displaced by federal projects. I am speaking of those people who already were caught up in a federal project involving dislocation at the time the bill became law early in 1971.

An example from my own Congressional District in Colorado illustrates the problem I am getting at.

Land acquisition for the Trinidad Dam Project under the Corps of Engineers in Southern Colorado caused the community of Sopris to be obliterated. Sopris was a little town back in the mountains of the South-Central part of the State. It once was something of a mining center but that activity has declined. Most of the people who remained there were elderly, former miners or the descendants of miners.

The necessary land acquisition for the dam and reservoir was well advanced by the time Public Law 91-646 with its improved relocation benefits came into being. Almost all of the 215 families that previously lived there had moved, receiving payments for their homes and property and such meager relocation assistance as was available under the old law. On the average they received between $4,500 and $5,000 for their homes. Those who qualified for any relocation aid at all generally got $400.

page two

But some twenty families remained in Sopris for a time after the new law went into effect and, consequently, they became eligible for the increased benefits. Twelve of those cases have been settled under the new Act and eight more remain to be settled. Those who already had left were not eligible even though they, too, in many instances needed the additional assistance.

I'm sure this committee is well aware of the hardships displacement often brings, even under the best of circumstances That was one of the reasons the present law was created. In the case of Sopris we're not talking about wealthy people trying to pry a few more dollars out of the federal treasury. We're talking about a few small businessmen and about 215 homeowners, most of them elderly, who had the misfortune of living in the way of a needed federal project.

They had to take the money the government gave them for their homes and attempt to find housing elsewhere.

Those who had been living in marginal or sub-standard housing had a definite problem under the old law. The money they received for their homes was not enough to begin to find safe, decent and sanitary housing so, in effect, they were driven from one sub-standard dwelling to another.

Many of the Sopris workers were employed in nearby Trinidad so they tried to move there, only to find prices for comparable housing well above the amounts they had received for their homes.

Savings were eaten up in some cases. Persons nearing retirement or already retired now face new home mortgage payments with very limited incomes. In short, the dislocation brought hardship to numerous families that could have been eased under the new law.

page three

The extra payrents of up to $15,000 for comparable housing
in Section 203 of the 1970 Act would have been very useful to many of
the families, but they had already moved and so, were not eligible.
Section 203 and other parts of the law were of significant benefit to
some of the families who remained in Sopris long enough to qualify.

Of the twelve cases settled under the new law, six of the families
received the same for moving expenses or replacement housing as they would
have under the old law --- about $400. One business received $4,809.96 in
relocation benefits. It would have gotten $350 under the old law. Another,
which would have gotten $575 under the old law, received $2,936.70. Three
families received increased relocation payments to help them find safe,
decent and sanitary housing. Under the old law they would have gotten $400
apiece. Under the new Act they received $2,425, $9,160.29, and $4,995.
I do not have the facts for the twelth case.

I am not here to cast envy upon those few who did benefit or to
say they should not have gotten the additional payments My point is that
this federal project bore upon every resident of Sopris at the same time.

The Corps of Engineers asked everyone to leave the town by
December, 1970. That deadline was prior to final passage of the new Act.
One hundred ninety-five of the families complied and, in effect, were
penalized for doing so. Twenty families could not or would not meet the
deadline and they are the only beneficiaries among the former residents of
Sopris. It seems to me that this situation points out a serious unfairness
that is written into the present law.

page four

I respectfully urge that this committee consider amending the Relocation Assistance Act to extend the benefits to all those people who were dislocated by federal projects under way at the time this law was signed.

There may be arguments that it would be difficult from the government's point of view to re-open cases of persons who have been dislocated. I would hope that such arguments would be weighed against the difficulties facing the people who have settled under the old law

I believe the present situation as I have described it represents an inequity that the Congress can and should remedy.

Appendix E

NEW SOPRIS INC.

The following pages contain the New Sopris articles of incorporation.

ARTICLES OF INCORPORATION
OF
NEW SOPRIS, INC.
Colorado Corporation Nonprofit

ARTICLE I

The name of the corporation shall be NEW SOPRIS, INC.

ARTICLE II

This corporation shall have perpetual existence.

ARTICLE III

The purpose for which this corporation is organized is as

follows:

To promote the building of a housing project in the County
of Las Animas, State of Colorado to re-locate the residents
of the Sopris, Piedmont and adjoining vicinity who are
being forced to move from their present homes because of
the construction of the Purgatorie dam project; and to
acquire by purchase, gift, donations or demise, and to
hold for the purposes hereinafter mentioned, real estate
in or as additions to City of Trinidad or within the
County of Las Animas, and to lay out and plat the same
into streets, alleys and blocks, and to sell and dispose
of the lots and blocks so surveyed, laid out and platted,
for the purpose of providing for building sites for the
members of this corporation.

ARTICLE IV

The address of its initial registered office shall be 210

First National Bank Building, Trinidad, Colorado, 81082, Las

Animas County. The name of its initial registered agent at such

address is Harry R. Sayre.

ARTICLE V

The names and addresses of the initial board of directors

who shall serve until their successors are chosen shall be the

following, who shall also be the incorporators of this corpora-

tion:

1. John Maccagnan - Route 1, Box 378, Trinidad, Colorado
2. Richard Morgan - Route 1, Box 389, Trinidad, Colorado
3. Louis Cunico - Box 213, Sopris,Colorado 81072
4. Crist Cunico - Route 1, Box 371A, Trinidad, Colorado
5. Jasper Butero, Sr. - Box 107, Sopris, Colorado 81072

BOOK 715 PAGE 516

ARTICLE VI

The by-laws of this corporation shall provide for the class of members or persons who shall be eligible to be members of this corporation.

Dated ~~May~~ July 27th, 1968.

John Maccagnan
Crist Cunico
Louis Cunico
Jasper Butero Sr.
Richard Morgan

STATE OF COLORADO)
                   : ss.
COUNTY OF LAS ANIMAS)

The above and foregoing instrument was subscribed and sworn to before me this 24th day of ~~May,~~ July, 1968, by John Maccagnan, Richard Morgan, Louis Cunico, Crist Cunico and Jasper Butero, Sr.

Harry R. Sayre
Notary Public

My commission expires August 16, 1969.

HELPFUL RESOURCES FOR ADDITIONAL RESEARCH

LIBRARIES AND MUSEUMS

Carnegie Library for Local History, 1125 Pine Street, Boulder, CO 80302 and at https://boulderlibrary.org/locations/carnegie

History Colorado, 1200 Broadway, Denver, CO 80203 and at https://www.historycolorado.org/contact-us

Pikes Peak Library District, PO Box 1579, Colorado Springs, CO 80901 and at https://ppld.org

Steelworks Center of the West, 215 Canal Street, Pueblo, CO 81004 and at https://www.steelworks.us/archives/collections

Trinidad Carnegie Library, 202 N. Animas Street, Trinidad, CO 81082 and at https://trinidadpubliclibrary.org

Western History/Genealogy, Central Library, 10 W. 14th Avenue Parkway, Denver, CO 80204

WEBSITES

Access Las Animas County Assessor Archive Site (a pay-to-view website), http://gov.arcasearch.com/uscolaa/

Ancestry, https://www.ancestry.com

Annual State Coal Mine Inspector Reports, https://spl.cde.state.co.us/artemis/nrserials/nr930010internet

Library of Congress, https://www.loc.gov

Newspaper Archives (often available remotely through your local library), https://newspaperarchive.com

The Statue of Liberty, Ellis Island Foundation Inc., https://www.statueofliberty.org/heritage-documents

The U.S. National Archives and Records Administration, https://www.archives.gov

Veterans' Service Records, https://www.archives.gov/veterans

NOTES

Introduction

1. Fred Beisser, "Richard Sopris," Find a Grave, https://www.findagrave. com/memorial/8679195/richard-sopris.
2. Ancestry.com, *"Civil War Soldier Records and Profiles, 1861–1865."*
3. "General E.B. Sopris, Prominent Figure in Colorado Public Life since Sixties," *Chronicle-News* (Trinidad, CO), March 20, 1913.
4. *The Men Who Built America*, directed by Ruán Magan and Patrick Reams. New York City: Stephen David Entertainment, 2012.

Part I

5. "Death Claims General Sopris," *Longmont (CO) Times*, January 30, 1936.
6. Fred Beisser, "Richard Sopris," Find a Grave, https://www.findagrave. com/memorial/8679195/richard-sopris.
7. Ibid.
8. "Daily News," *Rocky Mountain News* (Denver, CO), March 30, 1867.
9. "Death Claims General Sopris," *Longmont (CO) Times*, January 30, 1936.
10. "Treaties," *Georgetown (DE) Union*, September 22, 1865.
11. "Daily News," *Rocky Mountain News* (Denver, CO), July 9, 1867.
12. "Death Claims General Sopris," *Longmont (CO) Times*, January 30, 1936.
13. Patterson, "Confirmed, Etc.," *Colorado Miner* (Georgetown, CO), January 24, 1874.
14. "General E.B. Sopris, Prominent Figure."
15. "The House," *Rocky Mountain News* (Denver, CO), January 28, 1883.

16. "Firemen's Race Declared Off," *Weekly Register* (Baltimore, MD), August 20, 1886.
17. Kathryn Wirth, "Golden," Colorado Encyclopedia, History Colorado, https://coloradoencyclopedia.org/article/golden.
18. U.S. Bureau of Land Management (Department of the Interior), "Surveys." https://glorecords.blm.gov.
19. "Frauds in Coal Lands," *Rocky Mountain News* (Denver, CO), April 10, 1887.
20. "Score One for Sopris," *Rocky Mountain News* (Denver, CO), April 10, 1887.
21. Encyclopedia.com, "Land Scrip." https://www.encyclopedia.com/history/dictionaries-thesauruses-pictures-and-press-releases/land-scrip
22. "Those Lots Upon Which General E.B. Sopris Has Filed Script," *Rocky Mountain News* (Denver, CO), September 3, 1886.
23. Sopris and Bright advertisement, *Trinidad Enterprise* (Trinidad, CO), April 16, 1875.
24. Sopris plat, Las Animas County Archives.
25. "Paid Under Protest," *Rocky Mountain News* (Denver, CO), October 23, 1892.
26. Caselaw Access Project, "Colorado Fuel Co. v. Maxwell Land Grant Co., 22 Colo. 71 (1896)." https://cite.case.law/colo/22/71/.
27. "General E.B. Sopris, Prominent Figure."
28. Find a Grave, "Mary Louise *St. Vrain* Sopris." https://www.findagrave.com/memorial/28461931/mary-louise-sopris.
29. "Morrill's Marriage," *Sedalia (MO) Weekly Bazoo*, June 12, 1888.
30. "Missing Morrill," *Sedalia (MO) Weekly Bazoo*, October 1, 1878.
31. "Morrill's Marriage."

Part II

32. Interview with Elizabeth Antista DelMonte, May 23, 2016.
33. *Polk's Trinidad City Directory*, vols. 1904, 1910 and 1912 (Colorado Springs, CO: R.L. Polk Directory). Via Ancestry.com.
34. Access Las Animas County Assessor Archive Site, http://gov.arcasearch.com/uscolaa/.
35. U.S. Bureau of Land Management (Department of the Interior), https://glorecords.blm.gov/details/patent/default.aspx?accession=CO1180__.189&docClass=STA&sid=0qwkl5bq.2uh.
36. "Christmas Diocesan Review Edition," *Denver Catholic Register*, December 21, 1911. https://archives.archden.org/islandora/object/archden%3A2478.

37. "The Blaine Movement," *Silver Standard* (Silver Centre, Clear Creek County), May 12, 1888.
38. "Consolidation of the Colorado Fuel Company and the Denver Fuel Company," *Rocky Mountain News* (Denver, CO), February 25, 1889.
39. *Third Biennial Report of the State Inspector of Coal Mines of the State of Colorado for the Years of 1887–1888.* Denver: Collier and Cleveland Lith Co., State Printers, 1889. https://spl.cde.state.co.us/artemis/nrserials/nr930010internet/nr930010188788internet.pdf.
40. "Consolidation"; "Paid Under Protest," *Rocky Mountain News* (Denver, CO), October 23, 1892.
41. United States Census Bureau.
42. Interview with Charles Cambruzzi, June 2016.
43. Charles spells his surname with an *o*.
44. Interview with Charles Martorano, September 2015.
45. Interview with Lois Terry Mantelli, September 2022.
46. "$10,000 Fire Loss Sopris Last Night," *Walsenburg World* (Walsenburg, CO), August 1, 1924.
47. Interview with Charles Cambruzzi, June 2016.
48. Interview with John Cunico, September 2015.
49. Interview with Bernadine Martorano Kells, June 2016.
50. "Condensed News," *Castle Rock Journal* (Castle Rock, CO), August 16, 1882.
51. *Third Biennial Report.*
52. "Trinidad Items," *Rocky Mountain News* (Denver, CO), January 19, 1888.
53. "The Colorado Supply Company," *Camp and Plant*, March 26, 1904. http://steelworks.us/wp-content/uploads/2015/09/CP_1904_03_26_V5N11.pdf.
54. Ibid.
55. Sopris Plat, Access Las Animas County Assessor Archive Site, http://gov.arcasearch.com/uscolaa/.
56. "Consolidation."
57. "Paid Under Protest."
58. V. Butsch, L.C. Paddock, C.A. Butsch, "John D. Rockefeller Has Bought the Colorado Fuel & Iron Company," *Boulder (CO) Daily Camera*, June 25, 1903.
59. Ibid.
60. "Pity the Rich Man," *Salida (CO) Record*, November 27, 1903.
61. "C.F.&I. Company New Directors," *Silver Cliff (CO) Rustler*, August 26, 1903.

62. Charlotte Teller, "Behind the Colorado Coal Strike," *Pueblo (CO) Labor Advocate*, February 12, 1904.

63. "Mitchell Is at Trinidad," *Pueblo (CO) Labor Advocate*, December 4, 1903.

64. "Troops Sent to Trinidad," *Telluride (CO) Journal*, March 24, 1904.

65. In other words, a higher rate for each pound/ton of coal they put in the ore car; for instance, 35 instead of 30 cents per pound. Miners only got paid for the amount of coal in the ore car, so if you spent half your day building the wooden framing to support the roof so it didn't fall in, you earned nothing for those hours. Likewise, if you were blasting to open the coal seam, it wasn't going to be money until it went into the ore car—and you had to be sure it did not contain any of the surrounding rock, just pure coal. This is what was meant by "dead work": things that you had to do but that kept you from putting coal into your ore car during the hours you were doing them.

66. "A History of the Colorado Coal Field War," Colorado Coal Field Project, Denver University, https://www.du.edu/ludlow/cfhist2.html.

67. "Carlson and Ammons to Be Witnesses at Probe," *Chronicle News* (Trinidad, CO), November 30, 1914.

68. Kirk Hallahan, "Ivy Lee and the Rockefellers' Response to the 1913–1914 Colorado Coal Strike," *Journal of Public Relations Research* 14, no. 4 (October 2002): 265–315. DOI: 10.1207/S1532754XJPRR1404_1.

69. Andy Archuleta, comment on Sopris Reunion Facebook page, 2022, https://www.facebook.com/media/set/?set=a.120606202589736&type=3.

70. Interview with Nick Furia, June 2016.

71. Interview with Dora Faldutto, September 2016.

72. Access Las Animas County Assessor Archive Site, http://gov.arcasearch.com/uscolaa/.

73. "Capt. Frost of State Guard Shows Class of Men in Charge of Coal Strike," *Chronicle-News* (Trinidad, CO), August 26, 1914.

74. "Shots Echo in Hills," *Elk Mountain Pilot*, November 6, 1913.

75. "The Crimes of a Union," *Chronicle-News* (Trinidad, CO), August 27, 1914. https://digitalcollections-baylor.quartexcollections.com/Documents/Detail/waco-morning-news-waco-texas-vol.-3-no.-143-saturday-march-7-1914/542864

76. "Coal Miner Says Acted Dual Role," *Waco (TX) Morning News*, March 7, 1914. https://digitalcollections-baylor.quartexcollections.com/Documents/Detail/waco-morning-news-waco-texas-vol.-3-no.-143-saturday-march-7-1914/542864.

77. Interview with Robert Cunico, August 1, 2019.

78. "House Cat's Bite Proves Fatal for Sopris Grocer," *World Independent* (Walsenburg, CO), July 22, 1937.

79. Interview with Robert (Bob) Cunico, August 2020.

80. U.S. Census Bureau, https://www.census.gov/data.html.

81. *Eleventh Biennial Report of the State Coal Mine Inspector 1903–1904* (Denver, CO: Smith-Brooks Printing Company, State Printers, 1905).

82. Doug Conarroe, *Lost Lafayette Colorado* (Charleston, SC: Arcadia Publishing, 2021).

83. "Rocky Mountain Fuel Company," https://ourfamilyhistoryblog.files.wordpress.com/2012/09/rocky-mountain-fuel.pdf.

84. Vassar Encyclopedia, "Josephine Roche 1908," https://vcencyclopedia.vassar.edu/distinguished-alumni/josephine-roche/.

85. "R.M. Fuel Co. Is Dickering for Big Property, Report," *Chronicle-News* (Trinidad, CO), November 21, 1915.

86. Book 448, page 479, Access Las Animas County Assessor Archive Site, https://gov.arcasearch.com/uscolaecd/.

Part III

87. *Santa Fe Daily New Mexican*, September 26, 1875.

88. *Colorado Springs Weekly Gazette*, February 12, 1881.

89. *Cincinnati Commercial Gazette*, April 22, 1886.

90. *Dunkirk Lake Shore Observer*, August 20, 1886.

91. *Springfield Herald*, June 12, 1903.

92. *Colorado Springs Weekly Gazette*, October 6, 1904.

93. *Canon City Record*, July 16, 1908.

94. *Los Angeles Herald*, August 20, 1909.

95. *Chronicle-News*, July 23, 1914.

96. *Wichita Daily Times*, July 23, 1925.

97. *New Castle News*, April 24, 1942.

98. *Greeley Daily Tribune*, July 23, 1954.

99. *Greeley Daily Tribune*, May 19, 1955.

100. *Santa Fe New Mexican*, June 17, 1965.

101. Interview with Charles Martorano, superintendent, Southern Division, C&W Railroad, May 2021.

102. World Biographical Encyclopedia, "J. Edgar Chenoweth," https://prabook.com/web/j.edgar.chenoweth/6874.

103. "Dreams and Disappointments," *Pueblo (CO) Chieftain*, May 16, 2010. https://www.chieftain.com/story/opinion/2010/05/16/dreams-disappointment/8737132007.
104. Minutes of the Arkansas River Compact Administration Annual Meeting, December 14, 1954, Lamar, Colorado.
105. "Army Engineers Make Visit to Proposed Sites of Dams," *Chronicle-News* (Trinidad, CO), September 9, 1937.
106. *Chronicle-News*, September 9, 1937.
107. *Estes Park Trail*, January 2, 1953.
108. *Greeley Daily Tribune*, January 2, 1954.
109. *Greeley Daily Tribune*, June 22, 1954.
110. *Greeley Daily Tribune*, October 27 and 28, 1954.
111. *Greeley Daily Tribune*, May 25, 1956.
112. *Greeley Daily Tribune*, June 22, 1956.
113. *Greeley Daily Tribune*, February 18, 1957.
114. *Greeley Daily Tribune*, July 9, 1958.
115. *Colorado Springs Gazette*, January 20, 1961.
116. *Colorado Springs Gazette*, January 11, 1963.
117. *Greeley Daily Tribune*, June 11, 1963.
118. *Greeley Daily Tribune*, April 29, 1964.
119. *Colorado Springs Gazette*, April 22, 1967.
120. *Colorado Springs Gazette*, May 14, 1967.
121. *Colorado Springs Gazette*, August 18, 1968.
122. *Greeley Daily Tribune*, October 30, 1977.

Part IV

123. James Dalrymple, *10th Annual Report of the State Inspector of Coal Mines* (Denver, CO: Eames Brothers, 1923), 54–57.
124. Fundamental Statute of the Societá Fratellanza Operaia di M. S. of Sopris Las Animas County, Colorado, U.S.A. (New York: Stamperia del "Bollettino," 178 Park Row).
125. Ibid.
126. Book 719, page 385, Access Las Animas County Assessor Archive Site, http://gov.arcasearch.com/uscolaa/.
127. Interview with John Sebben Jr., September 2015.
128. Interview with Tano Zamburelli, November 2020.

129. Interview with Robert Cunico, August 2019.

130. Interview with Charles (Chuck) Cambruzzi, June 2016.

131. "History of Diocese," *Denver Catholic Register*, December 21, 1911. https://archives.archden.org/islandora/object/archden%3A2478.

132. "Article in Magazine Tells of Jesuit's Credit Union Work," *Denver Catholic Register*, August 3, 1944. https://archives.archden.org/islandora/object/archden%3A6542/datastream/OBJ/view.

133. "Fr. Joseph S. Haller of Trinidad Seeks Chaplaincy in Navy," *Denver Catholic Register*, August 12, 1943. https://archives.archden.org/islandora/object/archden%3A7145/datastream/OBJ/view.

134. "Trinidad Jesuit Released from Naval Service," *Southern Colorado Register*, March 29, 1946. https://archives.archden.org/islandora/object/archden%3A112/datastream/OBJ/view.

135. "Jesuit Transferred to Kansas City Parish," *Southern Colorado Register*, August 21, 1964. https://archives.archden.org/islandora/object/archden%3A667/datastream/OBJ/view.

136. "Administrators Named Pastors," *Southern Colorado Register*, July 9, 1965. https://archives.archden.org/islandora/object/archden%3A780/datastream/OBJ/view.

137. Conversation with Ernie Montoya, 2021.

138. Conversation with Joyce Lira Anderson, 2018.

139. Interview with John Cunico, 2015.

140. U.S. Census Bureau.

141. Interview with Dora Faldutto, June 2016.

142. Alfred Laiminger, "Then and Now—Years of This Century (At Least the Last 71 Years of It as I Remember)." Personal memoir, 2000. https://www.sopriscoloradoreborn.com/al-laminger.

143. "County Baseball League Is Found," *Chronicle-News*, April 18, 1913.

144. Interview with Chuck Martorano, September 2015.

145. Timothy Dodson, "Coal Ball," *NINE: A Journal of Baseball History and Culture* 23, no. 2 (Spring 2015): 53–67. DOI: https://doi.org/10.1353/nin.2015.0000.

146. Interview with Robert Cunico, 2021.

147. Interview with Charles "Chuck" Cambruzzi, June 2016.

148. "Post Ballhawks," *Fort Warren Sentinel*, June 9, 1944.

149. "Motor Hub Girls Win at Trinidad Friday Evening," *World-Independent*, August 24, 1936.

150. Lincoln High School Yearbook, 1943–44.

NOTES TO PAGES 153–162

151. Interview with Charles "Chuck" Cambruzzi, June 2016.

152. "Berthoud Girls Play for Title," *Greeley Daily Tribune*, March 14, 1935. https://access-newspaperarchive-com.trl.idm.oclc.org/us/colorado/greeley-daily-tribune/1935/03-14/page-10.

153. "Rehwoldt Is Top Athlete for Bruins," *Greeley Daily Tribune*, May 23, 1938.

154. Ibid.

155. Louis Fantin, *Legacy of an Italian Coal Miner* (Winnipeg, Canada: Art Bookbindery, 2012), 63.

156. "Collegians Aid County Prep Track Meet," *Trinidad Trojan Tribune*, June 2, 1944.

157. "Track Team Motors to La Junta Tomorrow for Triangular Meet," *Trinidad Trojan Tribune*, April 20, 1951.

158. Las Animas County records, book 715, page 515.

159. Personal correspondence from the office of the Honorable Congressman Frank E. Evans with notes of testimony enclosed.

ABOUT THE AUTHORS

Robert David Vigil Jr. is a member of the Trinidad Historical Society Board and employed at Trinidad Abstract and Title Company, where he is preserving the history of the area through land records. He is a Trinidad native who graduated from Trinidad High School. His family first came to the area in the early 1900s. In addition to his work with the above organizations, he is the administrator for the Trinidad Colorado Historical and Memorabilia Photos Facebook page. History and heritage have always been important to him.

Genevieve Faoro-Johannsen's grandfather came to the United States from Fonzaso, Italy, in 1913, and began his career working in the Sopris mine. Her grandmother was born in Sopris to parents who came to the United States from Alia, Sicily. They raised their children in Sopris, and her father returned as a math and science teacher, completing his degree after serving in World War II. Johannsen's first six years were spent in Sopris, and her grandparents remained there until 1970. Her family relocated to Pueblo when high school teacher contracts were not renewed in anticipation of the school's closing, but the family returned to Sopris monthly to be with the grandparents and for holidays and special events like hunting season. Johannsen graduated from Pueblo South High School and attended the University of St. Mary (Saint Mary College) in Leavenworth, Kansas, earning a liberal arts degree.